Mission in the City

Hopes and Dreams
My story

Shirley-Joy Barrow

Copyright © 2018 Shirley-Joy Barrow

All rights reserved.

This book or any portion thereof may not be reproduced
or used in any manner whatsoever without the express
written permission of the publisher except for the use of
brief quotations in a book review.

ISBN 978-1-725629-14-1
Contact: Shirley-Joy Barrow
belbarow@gmail.com

The author and publisher gratefully acknowledge the
financial support of Te Haahi Weteriana O Aotearoa
– the Methodist Church of New Zealand.

Philip Garside Publishing Ltd
PO Box 17160
Wellington 6147
New Zealand

books@pgpl.co.nz   www.pgpl.co.nz

Printed byCreateSpace

eBook editions also available

Front cover Photo – by Tony Bell

This photo of the Whanganui River was taken from the
place where the author spent many hours talking with
homeless people who lived in the bamboo. Their thoughts
and dreams helped to firm up Emergency Housing and
then Project Jericho.

*Wherever you are Kevin, thank you for your conversations
and your challenges.*

Photographs in this book are by the author,
Shirley-Joy Barrow, unless otherwise identified.

Contents

Foreword

I first met Shirley-Joy when she and her husband (Rev Tony Bell) came to see me in my Electorate Office at Mt Albert. Shirley-Joy wanted to raise concerns over the lack of adequate mental health services for people she worked with. An ordained minister, Shirley-Joy was working in the community supporting people towards a future free from harming themselves and others.

I learned that Shirley-Joy's early life had not been easy and that she had set about working for those who were disadvantaged. Her experiences made her an ideal person to be doing the work she was doing. Shirley-Joy had a big heart and a concern for people whom society would often rather not know about.

As Prime Minister and attending the Rātana annual celebrations, I met Shirley-Joy again and we chatted over a cup of tea. She was now the City Missioner in Wanganui. I was impressed with her tenacity and her sense of hope for the city and its people. As City Missioner, Shirley-Joy hoped to bring to people in need of the basics of life: shelter, food, hope, and love.

As the book reveals, with a team of caring people Shirley-Joy sought to establish safe accommodation, and to continue to provide food for those who needed it through the foodbank, including through Friendship meals and the Christmas Lunch. She spent time with homeless people in the bamboo by the Whanganui river and in the sand dunes, listening to the dreams and concerns of those who lived in those rough conditions. Shirley-Joy worked with those seeking freedom from crippling debt, helped sort out access issues with the courts, and assisted with many other complex issues facing people who were ill equipped to deal with them – the stories of the people she worked with in Whanganui, some shared in this book, make her dedication to them and meeting their needs abundantly clear.

I warmly recommend this book. It opens a window on what life is like for New Zealand's most vulnerable people. From the safety of our warm, secure, and well stocked homes, it can be hard to imagine the lives some of our fellow citizens are living. In Whanganui itself, there is significant distance between the wealthy and the middle-income earners and the truly homeless.

Mission in the City writes about times when the City Mission was helping unprecedented numbers of people by providing emergency and permanent housing, by feeding individuals and whole whānau, by providing drop-in centres for those in need of a friendly and safe space, and by offering budgeting services – all under Shirley-Joy's protective and fostering eye.

The book tells of how under a corporate model, the Mission's focus began to shift. The humanitarian model which had been established began to erode. It ultimately disintegrated, culminating in Shirley-Joy's dismissal at Christmas 2011. This is the story of that journey.

Rt Hon Helen Clark,
Former Prime Minister of New Zealand, 1999–2008

Prologue —The Author

My life journey has always been filled with miracles. Some miracles appear in this book and some are for other books.

I am also familiar with times of struggle. Looking back, I never did very well at school and much preferred the company of animals to people. I loved the outdoors and music. My teachers said I was bright, strong willed and creative.

I faced the challenges of physical, emotional and sexual abuse. I enjoyed my imaginary and pretend lives in the forests, jungles, and the plains of the Wild West, all faraway places.

As a teenager I was alone and pregnant, and I was pressed to give up my first born son for adoption. This was something I would always regret. He was gone and a part of me went with him, I searched for him, but couldn't find him. I never forgot him.

I recklessly ran away onto the streets indulging in alcohol, drugs and unsafe relationships. I was always trying to out-run the pain of abuse and violence. I found out about my second pregnancy while on the streets of Auckland.

I was helped by some church people who ran a Christian Centre, and later was encouraged to go out and spread the Gospel. I married one of the residents there and we headed out with the fervour of new missionaries.

My second son was born, and I experienced a connectedness brought about by my deep desire to hold and raise him and not lose him. This marriage led me through a maze of heartbreak, and there were good times and tough times.

In Hamilton we founded the Anchorage rehabilitation hostel for young people, many from the criminal courts, those with mental health issues, and people struggling with addictions. My tasks were to cook, transport, and I was in a social work role for up to thirty young people.

It was here I gave birth to my beautiful daughter. Life was not easy being a young couple running a hostel, with two children under five.

We then welcomed to our family our first foster child. A 15 year old girl who desperately needed a family. I was only 21 years old.

I would continue to foster children on and off until 2010, mostly teenagers who could not continue to live with their families or needed some time away.

The years at Anchorage living in the public limelight, speaking at churches all over New Zealand, and running the two hostels were difficult. This took a toll on our relationship and the marriage ended with my husband leaving the country.

I moved back to Te Puke with my children and it was them that made life worth living. I had to fight to keep them with me when my husband tried to abduct them and take them to Australia. This was the catalyst for me to advocate for legal constraints on children being taken out of the country without any discussion or consent by both parents.

It took me several more relationships to realise how little value I had for myself, and how much I was drawn into manipulative and abusive relationships with men thinking that I could fix them.

I was always a good worker and often had several part time jobs, even when raising a family. I volunteered in agencies that served the community, enjoyed seven years as a volunteer ambulance driver / attendant with St John, worked in rest homes, and in the kiwifruit industry.

I began some formal training, a Certificate in Community Social Work and some short courses including self-development, holistic health, and massage. I tried my hand at some university papers but found my lack of schooling and dyslexia made this difficult. I did anything I could to get myself off the Domestic Purposes Benefit and into the work force.

I had a horse and cart and would take people to do their grocery shopping, mostly older people who remembered those days. We decorated it for kiwi fruit festivals and Christmas parades. My children and I would go out to groups in fancy dress and give rides, many enjoyed the experience.

I drove school buses and ambulances, worked in orchards during the kiwi fruit season, looked after other people's children, cleaned houses, and worked in aged care where I ran activity programmes.

I saw a need and wondered why someone didn't do something, and then I realised I was that someone. I often saw how something could be, and then set about enthusing others and forged ahead to make it happen.

With some supportive people we set up Sela Trust, a halfway house for abused women, men and their families and the Te Puke District Youth Trust, a place for young people to drop in and get help and support.

As an adoptee I always felt that I didn't fit in and had a yearning to find out who I really was. I was involved in pushing for changes to the Adoption Act to allow adopted children and birth parents to get information, when both parties wished to do this. Once the Adoption Act was changed and with the help of Rev Keith Griffiths, I met my birth mother and her family. What I had experienced as rejection for 35 years was in fact deep agonising love.

Seeing my adoptive and birth mother together in tears and hearing their stories, helped me understand how one reluctantly gave me up and the other feared she would lose me without the signed court papers. I began to feel somewhat complete, like a jigsaw where the pieces begin to make a picture. I trained as an Adoption Counsellor helping other people make similar connections with missing family.

From the Methodist Church in Te Puke I felt a call to Ministry and trained as a Deacon – a community facing ministry of service, graduating in 1988 and was Ordained at Palmerston North in 1989.

That same year my son left school to start an apprenticeship and my daughter planned to go to Wesley College as a sponsored boarder in 1990.

I moved to Matamata to help the Union Parish, who along with the community to set up a Community Trust.

With many people struggling to manage their finances and feed their families they were further impacted by the "Mother of all Budgets" (1991), which saw benefits cut and some people struggle to make ends meet, and foodbanks became necessities in most towns and cities around New Zealand.

After a time of working together and a night listening to jazz, the Minister at the church and I fell in love. Tony and I got engaged and began our married life together in 1992, at church on a day set aside to celebrate the founder of Methodism, John Wesley (quite appropriate we thought, for two Methodist Ministers).

The son I had given up for adoption attained the age at which he could search for me. I had left information for him to contact me and we met. No words can describe that meeting. I met his wife and in later years welcomed two wonderful granddaughters into our family.

In Matamata I worked part-time for the Churches Education Commission, training chaplains for schools and travelling around the North Island visiting schools and placing chaplains.

I completed Child Protection Training, attended a number of courses run by Doctors for Sexual Abuse Care. During this time, I worked with the Probation Service and Child Youth and Family (CYF).

Our Presbyter and Deacon Team ministry brought many challenges for us and for the church. Presbyters were stationed by the Methodist church and moved churches every 6–10 years. When they decided to move Tony to Auckland, they thought I would simply go where he went. However, there was still work to be done in training and equipping others to take over the work at the Community Trust, so I stayed in Matamata. Tony and I spent 18 months commuting between Auckland and Matamata.

Needing something else to do, I went speedway racing, which I found exhilarating. Racing with a class of men, building, racing and repairing my own cars, finding the limits of steel and my own courage; having my husband and children crew for me was amazing, as is a small shelf of trophies in the lounge.

In 1996 I moved to Auckland but did not spend much time in the church. I still felt frustrated by the church 'lifting' Tony and stationing him in Auckland when I still had ministry commitments in Matamata.

In Auckland I obtained work with the Safe Program, the Waitakere Probation Service, and the Paremoremo Maximum Security Prison;

I also continued training in counselling, family therapy, professional supervision and transitional ministry.

I continued to race speedway from Auckland most weekends during the season, traveling to Hamilton, Rotorua, Huntly, Kihikihi, and Matamata; I even travelled to the South Island to compete in the National title. I retired from speedway in 2001, sold "No 5 Alive" (as I called the re-built car) and I used the money from the sale to travel overseas to do research for the Diaconate of the Methodist Church.

I attended conferences in Australia and England, visited Scotland and Wales, Germany, and America – visiting New York and Nashville, then up into Canada to Toronto and over to Calgary.

In Calgary, we experienced the fallout from 9/11. I was so relieved to get back to New Zealand, I could have jumped out of the plane and kissed the tarmac!

Those three months overseas began a 10-year involvement with servant ministry as a member of the Diakonia World Federation. This brought together servant ministers, deacons, deaconesses and diaconal ministers from Europe and Africa, the Americas and the Caribbean, and the Asia Pacific Region, where I served on the Executive until 2012. I met so many dedicated people who selflessly served others, all around the world.

In 2002, we moved to Gisborne for a two year appointment as Presidential Commissioners. We undertook a Transitional Ministry – helping the parish to consider what future it wanted to have, and how that would work with the different cultures involved.

From Gisborne my daughter and I travelled to England to meet my birth father's family – three half-brothers, a half-sister and an aunty. My family puzzle was now complete, and I had a deep sense of belonging and knowing who I was.

I have always felt drawn to support people that came into my life and had a strong heart for those less fortunate than me.

Wherever Tony and I went, we were always aware of needs within our community, and connected with people struggling with their lives. We often had extra people living with our family and we would never turn anyone away who expressed a genuine desire to change their lives.

I believe life is about finding out who we are, what we want to do, and how we might do it. For me, it is less about why things happen the way they do, and more about how we handle ourselves when things happen. It is about how we treat other people.

I have interviewed a number people since 2012 who shared the hopes and dreams from their involvement in the Wanganui Mission (the Mission). It is with their permission I include their stories; some will be named and others not.

Many times in my life I have been blessed with people who encouraged and supported me through difficult times, and celebrated with me in successful times. Family, friends, colleagues, clients, staff members, volunteers, board members, those in other community groups and government agencies – all helped me improve my life. It is through their encouragement and support that I have found the courage to write this book.

As the Buddhist wisdom says, "When the pupil is ready, the teacher arrives." I have had many wonderful teachers and guides throughout my life, and they still arrive when I need support or have new lessons to learn.

This is my story.

Chapter 1 — A new journey begins

With our time in Gisborne coming to an end and expecting to return to the Waikato or Auckland where we had family, the church asked us to consider Wanganui. Although somewhat disappointed, we agreed to meet with the Trinity Methodist Church congregation in Wanganui.

While back in Gisborne we went online, looked for overnight accommodation in Wanganui and found a 5 star motel/camping ground. We booked in.

We arrived after a long drive and found our motel. When we checked in, the proprietor offered us the honeymoon suite. We asked, "How is it different from the other units and what was it like?" We were told that it was just like other units, unless we wanted some extras, battery things. "No thank you, no 'extras,'" was our slightly embarrassed answer.

The tiny unit we were shown had a red heart shaped pillow on the bed, and this was what seemed to make it the honeymoon unit, without the extras. The unit was far from 5 star and unlike any honeymoon suite we had heard of, however it was too late to change the arrangements made.

We stayed one night. Bignell Street Motor Camp and Caravan Park and its then proprietor were to become a well-known place to us as we got to know Wanganui.

We met next day with the church people who told us they wanted to reach out into the community and bring in new younger families.

We agreed to accept the church's stationing to Wanganui and spent our Christmas saying goodbyes, packing up in Gisborne and then crossing from the East coast of the North Island, with our belongings, to the West Coast.

I kept busy between January and July of 2004 doing some contracting with the Probation Service and my commitments to the Diaconate as the National Co-Ordinator, and my involvement with the Asia Pacific executive committee of the Diakonia World Federation.

In a local free newspaper – the *River City Press* a write up was done by Trevor Mackay titled *"Methodist pair an unusual duo."*

Methodist pair an unusual duo

BY TREVOR MACKAY

Tony Bell and Shirley-Joy Barrow are an unusual husband and wife team in Wanganui. Both have been ordained by the Methodist Church.

Tony is Trinity Church's latest Minister and Shirley-Joy is a Deacon. Rev Tony, in coming to Wanganui, has almost travelled full circle. He left his home town, Hawera, 40 years ago. He has had 30 years in the Ministry and, in the course of it, met and married Shirley-Joy.

He and his wife were presidential commissioners in the course of spending two years with Gisborne Methodists. They were there to take the parish through significant change, Tony said. Gisborne now had a Tongan as the main Minister, who looked after Tongans and the English speaking, and a Samoan Minister who looked after Samoans. "It was not easy for English speaking people," Tony said. "It was a letting go and handing over process. I understand the Gisborne people are very happy."

Tony did his training for the Ministry at Trinity St John's in Auckland, being in the first group of Methodist students to train with the Anglicans, in 1972. He has since served Methodist, Union or Co-Operating Parishes in both the North and South Islands, first at Cambridge and then at Ashburton, Kaiapoi, Matamata, Avondale, Gisborne and Wanganui.

He had found his time at Avondale stimulating because he had been a multicultural Minister for English speaking congregations. "There were probably nine-11 different ethnic groupings in the congregation. I enjoyed the diversity and richness each group brought."

Meanwhile, Shirley-Joy awaits another opportunity to Minister. It was ideal when they worked together, Tony said. "It's just a matter of waiting. She's a qualified social worker, counsellor and family therapist. I think she is probably enjoying having a wee break."

Shirley-Joy, who has been looking after grandchildren, said she met Tony in Matamata when she was in community facing work. They had worked together and found they had a lot of things in common. They had decided to marry after attending a jazz concert. Shirley-Joy was ordained in Palmerston North in 1989. Now in the Community Facing Ministry, which she had never really left, she had started as a detached youth worker before becoming

Shirley-Joy is pictured her grandchildren Jessie and Jade.

Tony Bell, whose wife is ordained, too.

involved in social work, counselling and family therapy. She had worked with victims of abuse for 20 years and more recently worked with sex offenders. She had been a street kid and a drug addict herself and "came that way to being part of the church." She has also been a speedway driver. She said she raced in Waikato a mini sprint openwheeler for eight years. Tony used to help her when he could, she said. "We worked together on the car."

Discussing Easter, Tony said it was the high point of the Christian year. "One of the essential things we may need reminding of is we are an Easter people. We are the people of the good news. 'The stone is rolled away. The tomb is empty.' I hope we (Wanganui Methodists) can live up to our calling as Easter people here."

River City Press.
15 April 2004

A previous minister who had been at Trinity Parish in Wanganui suggested I apply for the position of City Missioner. He said that this would be just right for me.

Wanganui (as it was spelt then) was a town-like city, or city-like town, with all the insider networks alive and well. As a new person to Wanganui I knew that it would take some time to be accepted, some say around ten years.

Looking around the city of Wanganui, I became excited about applying for the City Missioner position. It felt like the right job for me, a place to use the skills I had acquired along the way.

With historically high numbers of beneficiaries and unemployed in the city, I looked forward to finding an opportunity to work with the people I had a great passion for, people who struggled to make ends meet. I looked forward to working with volunteers and colleagues who also had a passion for struggling people.

By being part of the three Wanganui Methodist congregations in this city, I got to know some of the people in churches.

Sometimes, like the Whanganui River, this city flows lazily along, and sometimes it rages and breaks the banks. Like other small cities, Wanganui faced the struggles of poverty and wealth living side by side. Like the name change, some accepted it and some did not.

Some in this city were committed to helping others and therefore making Whanganui a better place. Some weren't, choosing to live in their comfortable places with their eyes closed to the needs of the less fortunate within this beautiful river city.

As the new City Missioner I was to build on the dreams of others who started Christian Social Services Wanganui (CSSW) and ran the City Mission (the Mission) in the 1990s. To dream possible dreams for the future of this small ecumenical Mission and the people who needed it most.

Chapter 2 — The prophetic predicts the future and dreams dreams

It is impossible to write about the Mission for the period July 2004 to December 2011, without being aware of the history and the amazingly dedicated people who brought the concept to birth.

So one of the first things I did when I started as City Missioner was read everything I could find about the setting up of CSSW. I talked to as many people as I could about how this amazing ecumenical venture had begun.

One of the things I know about religions and certainly about different Christian churches is this: although they have much in common, each is incomplete without the other. The quaint thing about denominations within Christianity, and interestingly in most religions, is that they struggle to see this. They endeavour to convince 'the others' that they, and only they, have all the 'truth.'

The Interim Trust's journey

In December 1990, the Christian Social Services Interim Trust came into being.

The final report of the chairperson of the CSSW, covering the formation time of CSSW was written by the late Betty Bourke CBE, QSM, JP, Papal Dame of St Gregory the Great and was titled "Go not to those who need you – but to those who need you most." *John Wesley – Founder of the Methodist Church*

The report gave her the opportunity, as chairperson of the Interim Trust, to look back and take stock of both achievements and failures. It provided the basis on which the organisation was built and the direction from which the growth of the trust came.

The vision was conceived by Maurice Woods, Andrew Doubleday, George Bowers and Kevin Morgan in 1990.

Mrs Bourke (who became a sort of midwife to this venture) spoke of,

> "Conception being the easiest part, with problems arising in bringing it through the gestation period to full term and a natural birth. Then carefully nurturing it until independence was attained."

The Interim Trust carefully researched the urgent needs of the community and the degree of support that would be expected; then promoted their ideas to their respective church groups and received "positive, active encouragement" and agreement to set up an ecumenical body, with three representatives from Wesley Social Services Board (Inc), Anglican Social Services (Wanganui) Trust and the Society of St Vincent de Paul (National Council of New Zealand). Each affiliated member was required to pay an annual levy of $12,000 in 1992, a total from the churches of $36,000. Those who served on the Interim Trust were recorded as:

- Anglican Social Services: George Bowers (1990–93),
  Miles Bockett (1990–93) and Heather Russell (1991–93).

- Methodist Social Services: Rev Andrew Doubleday (1990–93),
  Joycelyn Pratt (1991–93), Rev Gary Clover (1992–93) and
  Dr Alan Mangan (1991–92).

- Catholic St Vincent de Paul: Maurice Woods (1990–93),
  Michael Coleman (1991–93), Ray Osborne (1993),
  Betty Bourke 1990–93).

- They were joined by the Presbyterian Group of Churches in
  1993 which saw Brian George, Joan Worthington and Ray Laird
  come onto the Board.

With the addition of the Presbyterian Church this increased the churches' giving to $48,000. At that time Kevin Morgan was the co-ordinator from July 1991–June 1993.

The Interim Trust's objectives were to set the policies needed to reach their goals. These goals were: to put in place procedures to become a registered charitable trust, to appoint a co-ordinator, to take over the Anglican Social Services soup kitchen and day services, to identify and provide services which addressed the urgent needs of the disadvantaged in our community.

The Interim Trust recognised the work upon which they had embarked, as an ongoing process and needed a flexible approach to succeed.

The members were all very busy people, and it was said they met the challenge with, "excellent and unflagging attendance at meetings," and there was "determination to establish the Trust on a sound footing and attract other Christian agencies into the collective body."

The focus was on the foodbank and soup kitchen. It was a time when government legislation seemed to be punishing those on benefits throughout the country.

In July 1991 National's Finance Minister Ruth Richardson delivered what became known as "The Mother of all Budgets," which contained major cuts to welfare benefits, changes to employment law and new user-pays requirements in hospitals and schools.

It is interesting to note the then Prime Minister, Jim Bolger, rejected Ruth Richardson's Budget proposals. Ruth Richardson then appeared to undermine Bolger's leadership at every turn. This was followed by the famous Avalon Address by Prime Minster Bolger, which included these words,

> "I utterly reject having my Government driven by ideologues who know the value of nothing other than the purity of their imported theories. I completely reject these obsessed purists who put the balancing of the country's books ahead of balancing the nation's needs."

In May 1992 there was a major restructuring of the Department of Social Welfare into five business units including the New Zealand Community Funding Agency, Social Policy Agency, Corporate Office; along with the New Zealand Income Support Service, branded as Work and Income New Zealand (WINZ); New Zealand Young Persons and their Families Agency (CYPFA), which by 1999 became the Child, Youth and Families Services (CYFS).

Cuts to welfare benefits created huge problems for those on benefits. They were at the front line in the Income Support Services and there was a struggle to get answers to the growing poverty in many towns and cities around New Zealand.

Many people struggled to manage their lives and feed their families. In almost every centre in New Zealand a foodbank of some description became necessary. Churches were aware that some of these people would go around other churches getting help from each of them.

Interestingly, at the same time as this was happening in Wanganui, I was heading to Matamata to set up a Community Trust with very similar aims as the Mission. The foodbank there still remains active in serving the community.

The Wanganui District Council generously supported the work of CSSW, and this reinforced the outreach and mission of those churches by involving a wider cross section of agencies.

With the mission statement, "A Christian response to the social needs of today," the vision and long term goal of CSSW was to involve all churches in the region, in the provision of practical and supportive services. The aim was to encourage and stimulate self-responsibility and independence. This was expressed by the board in the saying, if you give a person a fish, you feed them for a day (foodbank); teach them how to fish and you feed them for a lifetime (life skills programs).

Food bins were put into churches and supermarkets, and service clubs were approached for assistance and grants were applied for.

In 1992 a 'Think Tank' brought civic leaders together to look at the needs of Wanganui. This was also the time when the churches' levy was reduced to $8,000 per church ($32,000 per annum).

As the Trust's work grew it moved premises several times. A decision was made to reimburse volunteers for travelling expenses, and a part-time volunteer foodbank manager and receptionist/officer worker were appointed.

Betty Bourke was very clear about the responsibility of the Trust, to encompass a "strong political responsibility to social change." This while the government of the time was withdrawing from its responsibilities towards people in need, it was the voluntary organisations who fulfilled an important social role in communities.

Her report was powerful and provocative.

> "Anyone of goodwill – any Christian or humanitarian has a responsibility to play a role in the formation of social and economic policy. The concept of compassion, justice, aroha and reaching out to others in the spirit of being part of the same human family must be given greater emphasis in national policy making today. The problems associated with unemployment and so many young

people facing a jobless future are not going to be solved overnight, so we must accept in this country the reality that services currently provided will be needed for a long time."

Betty Bourke's wish list included the establishment of a drop-in centre, the employment of a City Missioner to bring practicality to the city's care-giving, harnessing activities for jobless and aimless youth, and endorsing basic human values which must be given their rightful place in our Wanganui society. She wrote, "Caring, concern and justice are essential if we are to put Christ back in our society."

With twelve board members, each working within the five committees (finance, administration, public relations, social needs and property) which involved them in management tasks, the board set about work.

Fundraising was the responsibility of the board, later evidenced in 2012 a letter to the editor in the *Wanganui Chronicle*, from Life Member the (now late) Mr George Bowers, "As a Member of the Board when the Mission was established, care was taken to build up the monetary reserves to meet any emergency."

The 1992 strategic plan saw a project for 'aimless youth' put on hold.

The Christmas lunch was to go ahead but with diminished involvement of the then co-ordinator. The friendship centre at 243 Wicksteed Street closed immediately, and the foodbank was charged with establishing a structure for food parcel follow-up. The constitutional and bi-cultural commitment was to be discussed at board level. The decision on the night shelter/transit housing saw no action. A vegetable co-op would commence when a volunteer manager was recruited.

By 1994 the foodbank had moved to the Methodist Church and the Whare Manaaki drop in was opened. The City Missioner would provide social support, social information reports to the Community Development Committee, and a Chaplaincy Supervision service for the Mayor and Councillors and council staff. This was done through a community service contract which was reviewable annually.

The reporting involved,

> "...occasional meetings with the Mayor to discuss social initiatives, attendance at monthly Council Community Development Meetings, working with the Officer of that department and

> providing three written reports during each year, reflecting aspects of the social climate of Wanganui, social initiatives and developments and commenting on social trends with research on social concerns."

Church representation came and went over the years, however the late Betty Bourke commented, "There being no theological problems, all involved found the relationships very rewarding and they focussed on the positive outreach achieved and friendship with each other."

The 1997 strategic plan re-affirmed in 1998, with the late Brian George as Chairperson, was comprehensive. Mr George spoke of the pending termination of the first City Missioner's appointment at the end of July and the need for a replacement.

The emphasis of this plan was on maintenance of the present work, and ongoing training of staff so that the programs and services were strengthened. As a result, CSSW would be better able to meet real personal and community needs. Board members had one or more portfolios across the areas of CSSW's work, i.e. Whare Manaaki, foodbank, midday meals, Ezee meals, furniture, visiting team, Russell House, publicity and finance.

A training day, followed by a strategic planning process suggested, "To be successful strategic planners – Plan, Implement THEN Monitor and Review REGULARLY."

The next strategic plan I was able to locate was 2001. This plan hoped to achieve the following:

1. The employment of three full-time paid staff – City Missioner, Office Manager, Foodbank Manager and a part-time van driver/handyman.

2. Seeking where appropriate a financial commitment and support from the District Council.

3. Seeking the support of volunteer staff in several aspects of the work, volunteers to receive appropriate training under the supervision of the City Missioner.

4. Seek support of businesses and individuals with the ability to provide goods, services and financial assistance.

5. The continuation of a variety of established services available to those in the community requiring support and assistance. These now included foodbank, furniture bank, drop in centre, advocacy services, weekday midday meals (including Christmas day lunch), garden project, visiting team, van transport, Ezee meals, midday city snack venue, craft courses, male night shelter and monthly coach trips.

A plan in 2002 saw a move from a male night shelter to a wider focus, acknowledging the need for emergency accommodation for men and women, some with children. However, this was not included into strategic planning until 2006.

The two previous City Missioners – Rev David Pratt and Rev David Day are both now retired. In July 2004 I became the third City Missioner to work for CSSW and the first woman to be appointed City Missioner in Wanganui.

This part of the story begins with a change of guard with me as the new City Missioner. I had just one week with the outgoing City Missioner, Rev David Day before his retirement.

The board had also employed a new administrator (who also covered the reception area) as the previous one had left. With these two pivotal roles changing, the Mission risked losing institutional memory which I considered essential.

Rev David Day (City Missioner 1998–2004)

David spoke of when he took up the position, knowing the board wanted more than just a lay person to open doors to other churches. He said,

> "I did try to open doors, but the churches didn't seem interested, especially when it might cost them money. There were differences in theology that made it somewhat difficult. I did get to know the other clergy and that was very satisfying. It was one of my aims to bring the other churches together in the Mission, but I didn't manage it."

Some of his most memorable times were the midday meals and getting to know some of the people he would not have normally met, and they got to know him. He enjoyed Christmas lunches and finding a new location for Anne's Place (Whare Manaaki) and there were great memories of times with the Mission Travel Club (MTC).

Rev Day said, "It was all about the people who you knew to a degree were using the system, but not rejecting them because of that." He explained,

> "That some of the people around the Mission were difficult to work with and sometimes there were clashes, but mostly they got on. No-one got turned away, we found them a job as long as they were willing to do a job."

He spoke of the volunteers working lots of hours and their job satisfaction. The Mission gave some volunteers a opportunity when no-one else would give them a chance. He acknowledged he was not

Fond memories of days as City Missioner

By ANDREW KOUBARIDIS

There have been many highlights of David Day's career and he will remember his time as Wanganui City Missioner fondly.

David retired from his role as City Missioner last week and shared some memories with *Midweek*.

"Seeing the services develop has been wonderful – we've seen the drop in centre and learning courses expand, the furniture bank, and the midday meals which have become a place of friendship rather than survival," he says.

While the foodbank has seen a decline in the number of food parcel requests, there is always a strong demand for furniture.

"The biggest regret I have is being unsuccessful at drawing other churches to the City Mission. I'd like them to be part of it, rather than be outside it."

David would also like to see all the City Mission departments to be under one roof so they are easier to manage. "I'd also like the mission to be more visible."

After six and a-half years at the City Mission, five as a minister in Waverley, and seven and a-half years as Anglican vicar in Gonville, David has learnt a few lessons about human nature and Wanganui.

"There are good people at both ends of the spectrum, but we don't pay enough attention to people at the bottom."

He adds any society should be judged on how it treats its less fortunate, especially kids.

"I think Wanganui does well but many of the professionals in local caring agencies struggle to help those who're in need," he says.

"More jobs will help, there is definitely a correlation between unemployment, crime, and domestic violence."

After 50 years of getting up to go to work, David thinks it will be a challenge to find something to fill the day.

"I'll miss the contact because I love having people around but I'm learning pottery, and am the vice-president of the Jazz Club."

He feels extremely positive about Wanganui's future. "I feel Wanganui is the best place to live... culturally, scenically, with improved facilities. I'm staggered people aren't queuing to get here."

PHOTO: ANDREW KOUBARIDIS AK046027

Goodbye ... David Day stood down last week as City Missioner.

good at administration. He knew he got up some people's noses. With a smile he said, "I didn't ruin their lives and they didn't ruin mine."

In reflecting on his tenure as City Missioner, Rev Day felt he was more involved with people than his predecessor. He acknowledged that each City Missioner had gifts that were different to his. He moved around a lot and sat down with people. He was often out on the street, out and about.

In replying to a question about his contribution to the community as City Missioner, Rev Day said, "The relationship with Mayor Chas Poynter was a good one, he had a genuine interest in what we were doing. He turned up at the opening of Anne's Place."

Rev Day's experience of mayoral support and the links with the Council was a very important way of feeding back information about the social needs of the less fortunate of the Wanganui community.

Rev Day spoke of the strong emphasis on working with the Council. Providing reports to the Community Board identified certain council members who were very interested; Sue Westwood and Barbara Bullock, both of whom supported the Mission's direction.

Rev Day admitted that he never had much interest in funding. He felt that it was the board's job, but they left it to him and the administrator. He didn't recall them ever getting involved with the finances when he was there. He said,

> "Apart from the churches' levy, nothing else was raised and even
> the churches' levy was reduced over the years. Funding was a pain
> in the neck, but a necessary evil. Special people, like Betty Bourke,
> who didn't kowtow to Bishops, were strong and helpful, and people
> like Anne Murray – a caring Aunty."

David Day enjoyed the gentle nature of Brian George, and Dick Mansfield was a good strong hard worker. He spoke highly of a woman called Ngareta, and he was glad she was still on staff, saying, "I knew she had skills, but had never had them appreciated."

He noted that there were a number of sad people that came to the Mission seeking help, but they were all characters with their own stories.

Towards the end of the interview with David he told me that just because people are Christian doesn't mean you will get on with each other. He said, "People were having 'barnies' with each other, in the Mission and in the church, when it should be about peace, love and compassion." Rev Day was constantly amazed how people could eke out a living, trying to keep warm and clean.

While he was at the Mission the demand for social services was always there and was increasing with the economic downturn.

I recalled well his words, especially that he felt the Mission should be more visible and that there are good people at both ends of the spectrum, but we don't pay enough attention to the people at the bottom.

His parting words to me were: "Any society should be judged on how it treats it's less fortunate, especially children."

I remember writing in my first column in the *Wanganui Midweek* (a local free newspaper — 21 July 2004) Titled *"Genesis – a new beginning."*

My experience had shown me that following on from the work others have started, means getting to know the past and moving forward, and also valuing the work done by passionate and able people. This worked when those involved in the past were willing to trust the process, let go of what had worked prior, and allowing new directions to appear.

Genesis - a new beginning

Kia ora - greetings from the messy desk of the new City Missioner as I take up my new role from the capable hands of the Rev David Day.

Genesis, a Greek word meaning "beginning" - my genesis is tiny compared with the beginning of the universe, the beginning of the human race and the people known in the *Bible* as the Israelites,

My beginning is more like a fresh piece of paper on which I can join with a team of people, both paid and voluntary, who are part of Christian Social Services at the City Mission.

In my meanderings I thought a lot about Jesus as he prepared for his ministry. He went back to Nazareth to the meeting place on the Sabbath, stood up, and read from the scriptures:

"The Lord's spirit has come to me, because he has chosen to tell the good news to the poor. The Lord sent me to announce freedom for prisoners, to give sight to the blind, to free everyone who suffers and to say, 'This is the year the Lord has chosen'."

I come to this new position with some fear and trepidation. There are things I can do without a lot of worry and there are things that I will need to work hard at.

Change doesn't come easy, and yet one of the few things we can count on these days is change.

We will walk this way together with Jesus in our midst. Our hands are open to receive. Our hearts are open to give. Our minds long to learn. And our souls reach out to each other. This time is eternal time for us. And God will be our blessing. Amen.

Chapter 3 — Knowing the history

It was into this environment that I began the year of the 'honeymoon.' I envisioned how to take the next steps with this wonderfully diverse ecumenical Mission, continuing to help people find hope in a struggling world. This Mission may have been the only ecumenical Mission in New Zealand at the time.

None of what happens next was exactly planned, nor was it random. Being a Methodist the term "prevenient grace" was well known to me – a sense of God having gone before us, to prepare the way. I began to work at the Mission believing that I would not be asked to do any more than I could manage. I believed I would see the Mission continue to be a truly missional activity. For me this meant bringing to life the teachings of Jesus and living them under the noses of some who have yet to embrace them.

To do this I needed to side with the poor, speak up for those wronged, and to be a part of a kind and loving community. I would find myself in the all too familiar place of challenging and enthusing those people who had always been able to have and afford what they wanted, to give to those who struggled.

I wanted to continue the tradition at the Mission that saw those who ventured in offered a special kind of relationship. This is best described by the theologian Jurgen Moltmann, who calls this, "a new kind of living together," that affirms:

> "That no-one is alone with his or her problems, that no-one has to conceal his or her disabilities, that there are not some who have the say and others who have nothing to say, that neither old nor the little ones are isolated, that one bears the other even when it is unpleasant and there is no agreement, that, finally, the one can also at times leave the other in peace when the other needs it."

> *The Open Church, 33.*

I was always of the view that serving others was to do something based on the desire to help and not with selfish expectations.

The Mission team consisted of a paid City Missioner and an Administrator supported by 100 or so volunteers, some with many years of involvement with the Mission.

Rick's Story

One of these volunteers who became involved with the Mission through the Task Force Green initiative was Rick Surridge. Rick had been involved for many years, and his knowledge of the history of the Mission led me to ask him to write up a potted history. I had access to the census and Social Indicators, but he had the inside stories. I was very grateful for his work and we were able to employ him for a short time, as a research officer with a grant from the Ministry of Social Development (MSD).

At farewell for Rick, the passion and dedication that he'd brought to the Mission was clearly evident by the speakers and words shared. Thank you, Rick, for your work at the Mission, both as a volunteer and as Research Officer, not to mention the times you acted as Assistant Missioner, so I could take leave.

*Rick (3rd from right) at his farewell
with other volunteers and Board Members.*

There was a historic arrangement in place that reimbursed the most regular of volunteers for their travel to work at the Mission. 'Regular' meant daily commitment from morning till afternoon on several days of the week. The reimbursement was set at an amount a person could receive without it affecting their benefit.

It was always a challenge managing the Mission's volunteers, all 100+ of them.

There seemed to be no appointment process for new volunteers, so I spoke with existing volunteers and then wrote role descriptions for all of the voluntary roles within the Mission. With these role descriptions written and in place, I had a process to work with for new people who expressed interest in being volunteers. I was able to work through with them our Confidentiality requirements and our Code of Conduct, request permission for a police check, and set up a trial period in the area of the core services they were interested in. If there were sufficient numbers of prospective volunteers, group orientation days were set up.

I always kept in mind that the Mission was not a new missional development as it had focussed on the needs of the city for the last 12 years. During this time the board changed its structure from a management model, to employing a City Missioner to manage the Mission on the board's behalf and report to the board.

Keeping people informed and sharing stories was always important to me, and I shared many of the blessings and challenges we received in the City Missioner's Column in the *Wanganui Midweek* most weeks.

I also reported regularly to the Anglican Bishop, the Catholic Bishop, the Methodist Synod Superintendent and the Presbyterian Moderator. I spoke at events organised by service groups in Wanganui, schools and local churches, highlighting the services we provided and seeking support.

Some people thought we didn't work in the afternoons, but we were always there. I shared this with the board when questions were raised,

> "I have been the City Missioner for 30 days and marvel at the way the morning rush happens Monday to Friday and becomes rather quiet by 1pm. However, the time after 1pm was a good time to talk and catch up on things like reading, letters, mail and conversations with staff."

Each week a staff meeting was held in the afternoons, beginning with devotions, and initially this was well attended. We rotated between the Mission and Anne's Place and staff/volunteers were encouraged to lead an inspirational opening. Later this devotional time was mostly at Anne's Place. To encourage and affirm the work of volunteers, I added an award to be presented to the volunteer of the month.

A couple of the concerns early in my tenure were staffing and safety, at all of our sites. With the board's and the Trinity Trust's consent, I embarked on several changes involving the work space. First, we removed walls which created more space for interview rooms and ensured a quick exit in case of emergencies and gave extra viewing from the reception area.

A young man's story

A young man arrived in Wanganui needing some assistance. Now this was not unusual. He was unable to get a benefit, because he didn't have an address; he was unable to get an address because he had no money to pay rent or a bond. I became aware that he was a painter by trade.

Being a dab hand at building as well, I asked him if he had thoughts on the changes planned. He did and set about removing the wall, cutting a hole for the window and framing it up for the glazier.

He spent so much time with us that this became his address, and he then was eligible for a benefit. In a short space of time he went from being penniless and with no place to live, to getting into a flat. The Mission Shop gifted him basic furniture and a heater. He got an adult apprenticeship as a builder and offered his time on the weekends to work on any building jobs that need doing.

At the Mission, synchronicity meant the arrival of the right person at the right time. It was to be something I was always in awe and wonder of, and very grateful for. As a need was identified, so was the answer to that need; be it workers, materials, finance or time – some would say it was the answer to prayer, something a lot of us did constantly.

I had begun to get to know people from the many varied and diverse groups who support people in this city, and some expressed some energy for an opportunity to meet and get to know each other. So, a date was set for a lunch, BYO of course, and invitations went out to other groups.

This gathering allowed collegial support, necessary networking, and was in the best interest of the delivery of services to the community.

Like the Missioner before me I made the office a place where people could come and talk to me. I embarked on an open door policy, and made myself available to talk with board members, staff, volunteers, clients, people from other agencies, and the public.

I met wonderful people with all sorts of challenges in their lives, some of whom experienced great change from spending time talking. Some people just needed a cuppa, a chat and went on their way.

Chapter 4 — Following on

The Mission did not exist to 'make' people change, but to encounter people in their times of need. To stand with them, sit with them, and listen to them. To support them and help them find hope and be able to follow their dreams. Sometimes the most important things people who came to the Mission had was a desire for a better future along with their hopes and dreams of being accepted and loved.

The first of these people for me was Ngareta, the special person spoken about by Rev David Day. She was a volunteer who became part of the foodbank team a year earlier. She remembers the talk about me coming and there always a lot of 'talk' around the Mission. Her mind conjured up a large, formidable and bossy person dressed in black. I think she imagined someone like the vicar from the television series *The Vicar of Dibley*. In the time I worked with Ngareta, she really embraced a special kind of caring and worked in several different areas within the Mission. We will hear more of her story as the book continues.

The office space that I took over was dark, the books on the shelves were old and dusty, and the room was somewhat cut off from the reception area. The first thing I did was clear the office, shift furniture and bring things from home to make the office mine, as you do. I included a white board with colourful magnets and creatures that allowed me to sort my dreams into pictures and shapes.

I set the furniture in place so that the door could be wide open. I put up venetian blinds to give privacy and lots of light from the window.

I spent my first few months exploring the Wanganui community. I was new to this city apart from a little contracting with the Probation Service, and I had a lot to learn about the city's uniqueness. I found that some of the best bits of information were available from the Council, through the Social Indicators.

I spent time around the streets, at all times of the day and night, talking to people. I talked with people in church groups, service clubs, government agencies and non-government agencies, schools and especially with young people to see what was happening. I needed to know what was being done by other agencies and what exactly did this city need the Mission to be doing.

I planned the first year to be a time of finding a place to share my gifts and skills in this new community. I wanted to remain open and not have preconceived ideas about what was needed in 2004, compared to the 12 years before.

I introduced myself to the Probation Service in my new role and heard about the history of the local prison and the challenges of people being released into the community. The highest priority spoken of was the desperate need for accommodation for their clients either on remand, parole, or at the end of their sentences.

I found out as much as I could by wandering around the city. I saw what the city did well, and what it did not.

I learned about the Council and the other agencies that made up this unique community. I found it helpful sitting beside the river, feeling the strength of its flow, following its history as a gathering place for Māori from up and down the river along with its pioneering families.

I loved checking out the area's waterfalls, the beaches, and I was somewhat taken aback by the iron sands. It was so different from the white sands of the Bay of Plenty where I was raised and the Gisborne coast, where we had just moved from.

The black sand burned my feet. It was not only my feet that felt the pain of this city, my heart too felt the pain of the lost and the least.

As I experienced the social rhythms of this community and the unique nature of those living here, I got to know the cultures that lived here.

Most of all, I got to know the good things that this city had to offer. I listened to the heartbeat of the city.

I learned that Wanganui had a growing number of people on benefits, and opportunities for work, especially for unskilled people, were few. This meant our young people often had to leave Wanganui to continue further education and find work.

Local businesses struggled to thrive in this city although supported by those beneficiaries who spent all they had locally, they lamented others who were able to go to larger cities nearby to do their shopping.

It seemed that there were a good number of social work agencies and groups running programs. Successive governments had embarked on 'seeding' funding for new groups, but little funding seemed available for ongoing ventures.

What did seem to be missing was the provision of basic needs for safety, shelter, food, furniture and household goods, clothing, fellowship and hope. A place open 24 hours a day with a 'real' person to take calls and find a way forward, and offering hope.

The need for food was near the top of the list, but some people in the community had concerns that the Mission had historically been ripped off by a visible few and that there was no real poverty in the city.

When reading the CSSW's strategic plans from 1991–2004, I struggled to see evidence of where the community, other agencies in Wanganui, staff and volunteers had been consulted over what was working and what might need to change.

A small group of managers of other service providers in the community had begun to meet regularly and I found meeting with them very helpful, this allowed me to get to know who was doing what in the community.

On my whiteboard, in bold letters I had written this three-part question:

> **What did this community need the City Mission to do that no-one else was doing, that needed to be done?**

Each time I spoke with people in the community I asked them this question and noted their responses.

My life experience, social work, counselling training, being an Ordained Minister, along with my experience in non-government agencies was important for the role of City Missioner. The last two Missioners were Ordained Presbyters (generally parish focussed ministry), and my ordination to Diaconal ministry was historically focussed as a community facing ministry.

I found it a little frustrating in the first months that board members were deeply involved in some of the services offered, something I was not used to. I understood that my position was to manage the Mission and report to the board, as defined in my job description.

My understanding was that the governance role was to provide leadership, direction, set in place (in communication with stakeholders) a strategic plan, and make available the necessary resources to carry it out.

The board must be satisfied that the management team is doing its job in accordance with policy and resources, and if not, it needed to ask why.

Management's role was the day-to-day operation and is typically the job of a co-ordinator or chief executive and their staff and volunteers. According to my job description, management was the City Missioner's role, along with the training and empowering of staff and volunteers.

Working at the coal face I began to notice that the board members' ideas seemed a little out of touch with the needs we experienced each day. I took time to share this with the Chairperson ensuring any recommended change was well researched and had a clear rationale, enabling these to be shared with the board before any action was taken.

I became disheartened due to a lack of cohesion and I discussed this with the chairperson. It seemed wasteful for the board to employ me to manage the Mission and then try to do much of the work themselves. On the other hand, their involvement in seeking funding and ensuring necessary resources was lacking.

I assured the chairperson I was following the board's guide, set through a strategic plan in June 2004. I got busy with management tasks.

The other difficulty I had was that there seemed to be few, if any, governance policies in place. I was able to share this with the board members and we committed time to draw these up.

I also drew the board's attention to the lack of accountability for funding over the last couple of years. This had left us in a difficult position when seeking grants. I spent many hours in the first few months preparing the required reports, as the 2004 funding round had already begun.

I remember saying to the board when I received blank looks about resources and money needed to run the Mission, "If you ensured my salary, we could raise the rest of the money."

I have always believed that if we are doing the right things, then God would go before us. I believed God would provide all that we need, called "prevenient grace," and this was to happen many times while I was there.

A new chairperson was elected later in 2004. This chairperson's knowledge of governance policies for schools, enabled the drafting up of governance policies for the board. This offered the delineation needed and clarified the roles of governance and management.

One important discussion that the board needed to have was around Russell House which was initially gifted to the Mission. It was to provide a base should the current space not be big enough or not available for Mission use.

The house was used, rent free, by the Schizophrenia Fellowship for a number of groups under their umbrella.

The house was named after a previous board member Heather Russell (Mayor 1974–1983). Russell House had not been big enough for the work of the Mission for some years and I remember my desire to focus the board on the future and not the past.

So I brought this question to the board: was it good stewardship of the Mission's assets to keep this building and allow another group to work out of it rent free? It was understood that without this generosity from the Mission, the Schizophrenia Fellowship Wanganui Branch would struggle to provide the service they provided for those with mental illness and their families.

Over months of discussion it was eventually agreed that this property would be sold at less than valuation to the Schizophrenia Fellowship and the funds invested for the work of the Mission.

This year a new and very different Mayor was elected. It was said of the previous Mayor, Charles "Chas" Poynter QSO; that he was very people-oriented. Mayor Poynter had been in office from 1986–2004. When first elected as a counsellor to the Wanganui City Council in 1977, he was a bookseller (a business he inherited from his father), and he knew a lot of people. The position of the City Missioner was important to him and he actively supported the work done by the Mission.

When I was introduced to the new Mayor at his investiture, he told me that he had no need for the 'down and outs' in his city. He did not seem keen on a place for 'them.' He also suggested that his wife would be dealing with the Mission.

I was reminded of the words of Rev Day, when I interviewed him in 2012, where he referred to the new Mayor, David said: "I expect that Michael Laws wouldn't turn up at anything unless it was a photo opportunity." This was a strong indication that the Mission is an important place for some and a concern for others. The Mission was a bridge between those that had more than they need and those who had less.

Six months into the job and I had begun to feel the stretch that being City Missioner would have for me, the honeymoon was over, and the serious work had begun. I was becoming clear in my mind what to do next and I had amassed a huge amount of information about this city and the mission. I now had formed in my mind a process for enhancing this missional activity.

Chapter 5 — Beginning with an end in mind

Over the next months I changed the things that were easy to change and lived with the things that were not ready for change. Sometimes I struggled to know the difference. I decided early in my journey with the Mission to keep the focus on core services. I established processes that would allow people's concerns to be raised and dealt with.

The introduction of a code of conduct for all areas of the Mission's work, and role descriptions for each of the core services, brought clarity about tasks and hours for staff and volunteers.

The role of City Missioner was a busy one covering the areas below.

City Missioner Activities

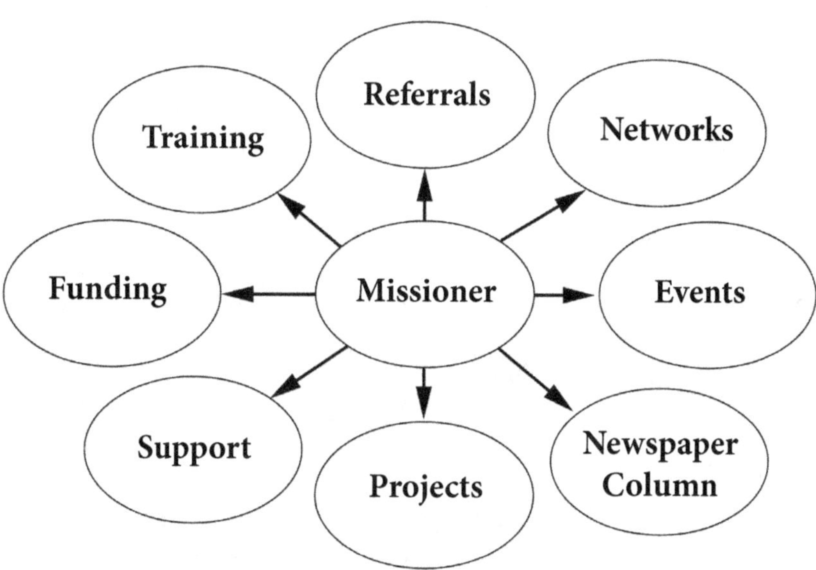

I was to experience a very diverse community when speaking at schools about the foodbank. Some students had no idea or experience of what those children who lived in poverty went through. Schools such as Collegiate and Cullinane encouraged their students to collect food and helped with the annual food drive, giving them an experience of the plight of others less fortunate than themselves.

The Mission had a working relationship with Community Probation, and we often welcomed new people who would spend a few weeks working with us to complete their community-based sentences.

I was enjoying working with a group of younger people who themselves understood hardship. They were a dedicated bunch and responded to my challenges and requests for them to handle the often demanding work of the Mission.

Ngareta's Story

A special people for me was Ngareta. She was told about the Mission by a friend and had come for food for her children at a time when her partner spent most of their money on other things. She found herself accepted at the Mission. No-one judged her for being in a stressful relationship.

Ngareta and her beautiful youngest daughter Mystery

She felt so at home that soon after her first visit for food, she asked if she could help out and took on the task of bagging rice, flour and sugar and putting food parcels together for others who came to the Mission. This was the beginning of an amazing journey into many life experiences for her. She did for the Mission what the Mission had done for her.

Being a solo mum, it was easy for Ngareta to empathise with people that came to the Mission. She was a willing volunteer and her commitment saw her become an integral part of the Mission.

I recommended to the board that Ngareta be encouraged to drive the mission van. My truck driving experience had taught me that one main driver would lessen the damage to the van. We supported her financially to get her full licence and I was able to coach her in backing and managing a trailer. We had many adventures.

Certain areas of the Mission were working well, yet some areas could work better. It was important to me that all changes were evidenced-based and in consultation with the community groups we worked with, then agreed by the CSSW Board.

At the annual general meeting at the end of 2004 I reported:

> "For the future, I see the revamping of the furniture bank to contain a workshop, offering a place for people to work with wood ...which will then be sold in the garage sale which will run twice a week. Our MSD project, which may involve a revamp to the foodbank, will be reported in April and decisions made soon after. Project Jericho is in its research stage to determine the need for overnight accommodation in Wanganui. We plan to open between 4pm and 10am when people would be offered a light meal, shower or bath, a warm clean bed and breakfast in the morning. During this time, it would be possible to establish their ongoing needs. Funding could be gathered as a 'bed night' and the community invited to participate."

Peter's Story

One day as I was sitting in my office, I noticed that the people in the reception area were rushing around and heading toward the staff room. As one person rushed past my door I asked what was going on. The answer came back: "Pete is in the Mission!" Pete, in the eyes of the staff and described by Ngareta was an: "evil, horrible, scary man… a patched gang member." I walked out of my office, expecting to see a large menacing man. Then finding myself a little confused by the frame at reception, he appeared to be a small man. As I ventured through the reception door I saw Pete standing in the space leading to the foodbank. His face was twisted and angry, veins rippling the dark tattoos. His hoodie was over his black hair and one hand was locked in a fist. He paced the small space like a caged dog. I chose to greet him with a hand extended and greeted him in Māori and went forward to hongi him. "Kia ora, kei te pēhea koe. My name is Shirley-Joy and I am the new City Missioner, would you like a cup of coffee?" He smiled a sly smile, "I'm Peter Karatau, milk and two sugars," he replied.

There was expectation in his voice, as if I should know him, as if everyone knew of Peter Karatau.

Peter challenging and stern

No-one had warned me of this small yet giant of a man. However, I was comfortable with my ignorance. I was excited to get to know him, and we sat on the couch with a coffee and we began to talk. This was the beginning of an amazing friendship and a journey we would both value.

As I talked with Pete, I began to realise this was no ordinary fellow. His experience and knowledge of legislation and his propensity to get himself into trouble, was only over-shadowed by his life story of abuse, incarceration and loss. From his sense of loss of land from his people, to the rights of everyone to be treated according the Treaty of Waitangi and their Human Rights. Pete was as radical as I have ever known.

I learned this day that he travelled often, hitch-hiking around the area and wider New Zealand. Not everyone he met was able to comprehend this slightly built ex-gang member who turned up in the most extraordinary places and claimed his right to be heard. Peter would wander in and out of my life over the next years, sometimes alone and sometimes with the Police a few minutes behind.

On another occasion after rescuing Peter from a run-in with a local business and the Police, he asked me, "Why are people scared of me?" Thinking quickly, I asked him if he'd looked in a mirror lately. He snapped back, "I never look in mirrors." So, I asked him if I could take a photo of him, and he agreed.

On another visit over coffee and after I had it developed, I showed him the photo and asked him what he saw. "Pretty mean," was his answer. I agreed. I gave him the photo and suggested that might be what other people see before they get to know him as I have.

In the first weeks of December, nearing Christmas, Peter came in and made a comment about there being no Christmas tree. "Kids need a Christmas tree," he said in a grumpy voice. This amused me as I knew from what he had said before that he hated Christmas. I told him no-one had time to put one up, but if he would like to do that, I would show him where it was in a box and he could.

Later as I headed out to the staff room for a cuppa, I looked into the store room and there sitting on the floor was Pete, decorating a small tree with baubles and tinsel. As he looked up, into the darkened room came a golden light. Quickly I stepped back into my office, got my camera and asked if I might take another photo. He agreed.

I showed him the picture and he smiled a peaceful smile as he held onto the camera. "Can I have this?" he asked. I got a copy printed for him. When I gave it to him, he said, "I look different – happy." Here at the Mission, Peter was as much at home as anywhere he travelled. He carried these two photos with him for many years.

At the 2004 Christmas staff meeting we accommodated a large group of around 40 volunteers, staff, and present and past board members. The staff were given certificates of service, followed by a few humorous ones. Some visitors came from other agencies that we work with. These staff meetings, along with the volunteer of the month award, became quite successful with numbers averaging 20–30 each time we met.

I looked forward to an exciting year ahead and appreciated the support from the board and their willingness to accept the challenges ahead.

As this first amazing year came to an end, I found myself writing in the *River City Press*:

> "See the stars as you look through the clouds at night. All over the universe people see the stars. We don't see the same stars, but we all can see stars. Stars don't only lead people on their journeys, stars also point the way.
>
> Stars unite the people of the world, the rich, the poor, the intellectual, those who cannot read or write, those that live in high up places and those that live low to the sea.
>
> And when they saw the star that time long ago, the wise men rejoiced because the star lifted them above their circumstances and made them think, they chose to follow that star and met the Christ child.
>
> The stars today can do the same, lift each one of us and move us to do the same. To lift us above our current circumstances and have us think…. 'Whatever they have, I need it.'
>
> The wise men never went home the same way they had come and like them, once we have met Christ, we are made new, the old has gone and the new has come.
>
> So, when somebody asks you, 'What did you get for Christmas?' smile and tell them you got HOPE that gets brighter each day; JOY that is greater than anything you have had before and GUIDANCE for every step of your journey from today onwards."
>
> *River City Press 20 December 2004.*

As this year ended I reflected on the human stars I had met and marvelled at people's ability to survive incredible challenges in their lives and come up smiling. The tasks I had set myself were complete for this year and the future was looking good. However, there is never a time for those of us in the Mission to rest over Christmas. It was always a stressful time for families who struggled, and so we remained open throughout the Christmas and into the New Year with a small, dedicated group of staff and volunteers.

Chapter 6 — Being feisty and hard edged

One of my greatest delights was when my son, his wife, and their children moved to Wanganui to live. Being close to them and sharing my two grand-children's young years brought me wealth beyond compare. I spent as much time as I could with them and they taught me much about living again with a child-like enthusiasm. Some of this found its way in the Missioner's Column in the *Wanganui Midweek* column, in January 2005.

"My granddaughter sat still on my knee while we watched the evening news. She snuggled up to me and said, "I feel a little bit sad". When I asked her what she was sad about, she told me that it was because, "all the people were dying every night." I was suddenly aware that each night as she watched the news with us she saw, heard and watched the news from the tsunami. In her mind this was a new event happening each time she saw the news. No wonder she was a little bit sad.

I became aware that we each see this disaster from our own experience and through our own eyes. This forms our understanding of the events. On Sunday some people went to the sea and imagined tsunami sized waves and were reminded the mighty ocean belongs to no-one.

Some weeks ago, when the map of New Zealand was shown on the news and I saw that Wanganui was not one of the places that a tsunami would hit. I felt relieved, did you?

Did you then look at the places that might be at risk and think if you knew anyone in that area? Being an East Coaster I knew of many people within that 1–8 kilometre range from the sea, in the Bay of Plenty, Gisborne and Hawkes Bay.

There will always be people caught up in disasters of one kind or another. With the media reporting as quickly as they do we will continue to know about it within minutes of it happening.

Our minute of silence can become ongoing as we remember that for some people life is anything but a blessing."

Wanganui Midweek 19 January 2005.

Some people called me feisty and hard edged. If being lively, determined, bold and assertive was what they meant, then yes, that was me! I was ready to face any challenge. Others may have also experienced me as touchy, aggressive, a bit irritable and easy to anger. I confess at times I would prove to be some of these descriptions. At the Mission, I was often dealing with emergencies, real and perceived, and faced with unpleasant situations. I could not always hide the effect of them on me.

Having only scratched the surface of what this city was like, I again looked to the latest strategic plan the board had done in 2004. Under the mission statement:

> "A Christian response to the Social needs of today; bringing this joint venture of Anglican, Catholic, Methodist and Presbyterian Churches under the Registered Charitable Trust of Christian Social Services Wanganui the Trust aimed to work towards a caring society that embraced Christian values and ethics. The Trust also reaffirmed its commitment to assist individuals, groups and families who were suffering or disadvantaged, towards achieving fulfilment and self-sufficiency by:
>
> - Helping people identify their own needs where applicable,
>
> - Assisting them to set realistically achievable goals,
>
> - Assessing the means to achieve their goals,
>
> - Understanding individual and community needs so that the best possible services can be offered,
>
> - Involving churches and community groups in the provision of programmes and services, and
>
> - Liaising with other agencies involved in social change."

The Trust Strategic Plan saw a continuation of the established services of the foodbank, furniture bank, drop-in centre, advocacy service, weekday and Christmas Day meals, garden project, visiting team, van transport, Ezee meals, craft courses, emergency accommodation, travel club trips and a weekly firewood service, (the last two of these for low income earners).

These services meant searching for funding and making applications to funders. I sought commitment and support from the Wanganui

District Council, businesses, and individuals able to provide financial assistance. I was responsible for the selection, management and training of staff and volunteers, and monthly reporting to CSSW.

It was a huge task to manage an office manager, foodbank manager, and over 100 volunteers.

Some people had been on the board for some time, and at the 2005 AGM, Graeme Carter retired from the board after 10 years of service, with the last three of these as chairperson. From the minutes of this AGM:

> "Graham responded by stating that over the last few years he spent on average 1.5 hours per day on CSSW work and while he is retiring from the board CSSW will remain in his prayers."

June King also retired from the board, and Bill Murray retired from the furniture bank. Bill spoke of his long involvement with CSSW and wished the organisation God's Blessing. Bill and Anne Murray had for many years been involved on the board and in the travel club, Anne's Place (previously Whare Manaaki) and the furniture bank.

With my first AGM over, I continued to look at the areas that the Mission worked in. Drawing from my training and experience, it seemed that the Mission was focussed on meeting the physiological needs of people. It was the presenting need of each person that we endeavoured to meet, and then link then into either one of our services or another agency within the community.

I believe the worker is worthy of their hire, and thus began moving certain roles from voluntary to paid staffing; the main roles where people were expected to manage volunteers and people doing their community service hours were funded first.

The younger people who were now working at the Mission were a very committed bunch. Many of these people had experienced much of what those drawn to the Mission had experienced. They deserved paid employment, due to the work they did and also to support their families.

Most of the people who came to the Mission sought the basics: food, shelter and clothing, closely followed by a need to feel safe and secure. Some people needed help to manage their finances or relationships – often with family, other agencies, and government departments.

Always in the background was their desire for belonging, hope and love.

To me, this resembled the bottom three levels on Maslow's Theory, a psychological theory regarding human needs.

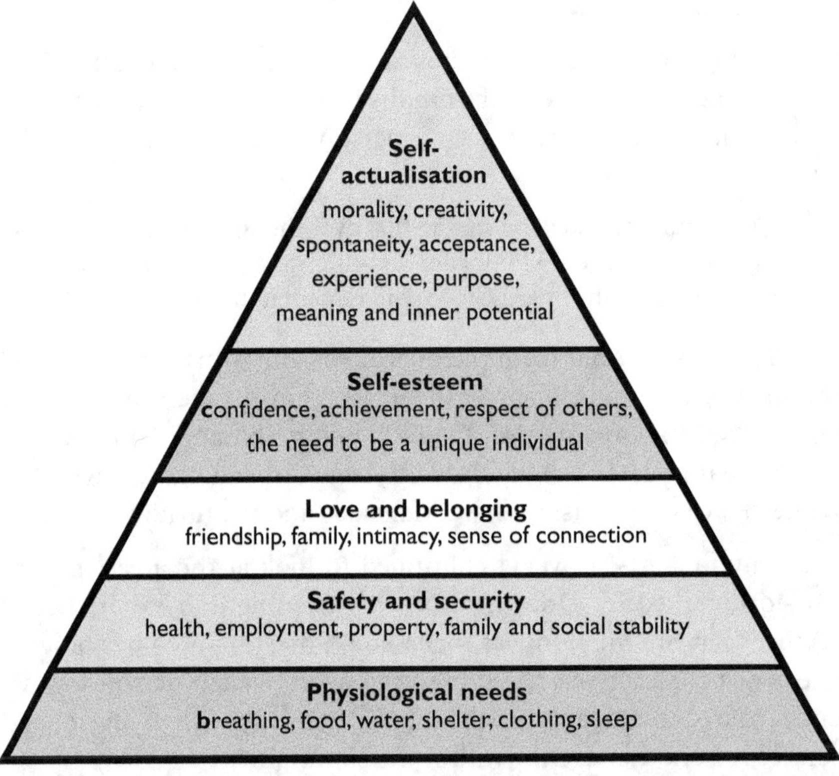

I believe that without physiological needs (bottom tier) being met, a person cannot function properly and will ultimately fail. If people do not feel safe and secure (second tier) they cannot thrive and if they feel insecure either personally, financially or because of health issues, they cannot easily feel loved and find a place to belong. Belonging and love are important, especially in childhood, but also for adults.

I noticed how many of the physiological needs for survival fitted into the services that the Mission was already providing or might do in the future.

Other agencies seemed to focus their work on the top two levels of Maslow's Theory and they saw the Mission as an emergency response focussed on the bottom three levels.

The board accepted the rationale for the core services based on Maslow's Theory in 2005 and began to see how the Core Services linked and worked together.

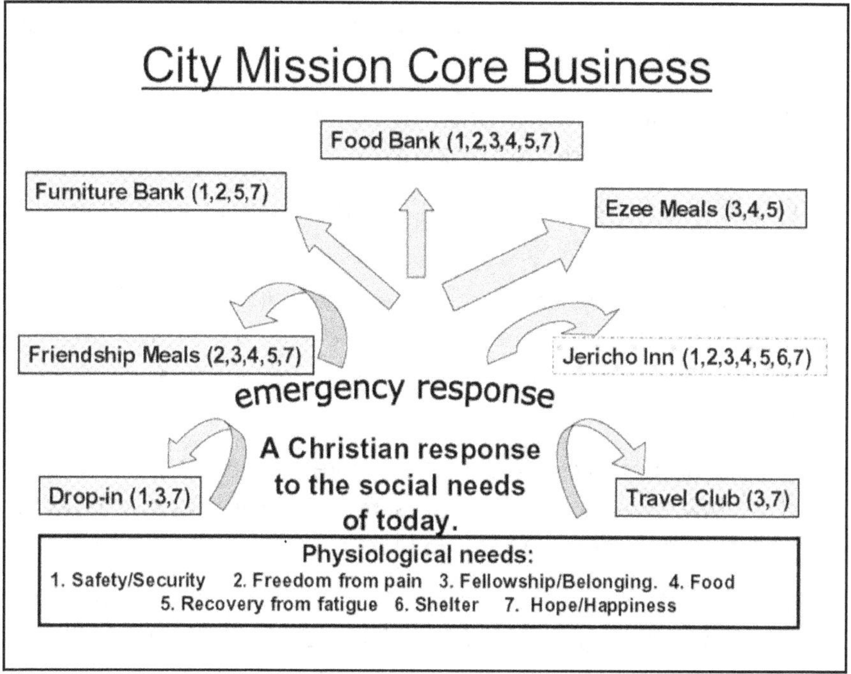

I presented my reports in this format to the board as a visual of how core services would meet each of the lower three levels in Maslow's Theory. This was also discussed with the Council's Community Committee.

The next step was to clearly demonstrate how the process worked when people came to the door of the Mission.

This began with an interview at the Mission Office – to assess and define the need in the areas of the Mission Core Services and or referral to other agencies within the community.

The areas of need assessed were:

- **Safety:** Call Police or if domestic violence – call Refuge and establish the degree of emergency.

- **Accommodation:** Establish emergency. If Project Jericho available decide bed nights, cost and go through House Rules, escort to the Project and introduce to the Manager. If no availability, contact other providers and agencies for long term accommodation.

- **Food:** Record income source and use. Clarify size and frequency of food parcels. Inform about Friendship Meals days and venues.

- **Furniture or household goods:** List priority items needed. Contact shop manager for availability, arrange delivery time and cost if any.

- **Power, Heating and Travel:** Obtain permission to access Missioner's discretionary account.

- **Fellowship or Friendship:** Offer Anne's Place and friendship meals.

The interview process established contact and began a relationship between the mission staff member and the person seeking help. Each of core services linked with the others when needed. (See Interview decision chart.)

Once the rationale was clear for the core services, then decisions could be made about the historic services we would continue, do differently, and those we might no longer do.

An example of those we would no longer continue was the Cans Music Festival, where the Mission was the recipient of canned food given as a door entry by the many students and their families attending the concert. The concert was part of the yearly school curriculum and met their requirement to be part of a performance.

The next area discussed was the visiting team (called 'The Extra Mile') – where a couple of wonderful ladies would go out and visit people in their homes and support them in whatever ways they could.

These ladies had done this for some time and saw the change in the Mission staffing as an opportunity to step down. The service stopped as no-one was willing to carry on these home visits. The safety of those visiting concerned me, especially when I heard some of the embarrassing moments and set-ups used by those visited.

We were available to help people when they found their way to the Mission, interview them and assess what they needed and provide for them. We simply sat with them, often over a cuppa or a meal and listened to their story. We didn't judge them, just listened as they told us how they had got into the situation they were in and how desperate they were to get help.

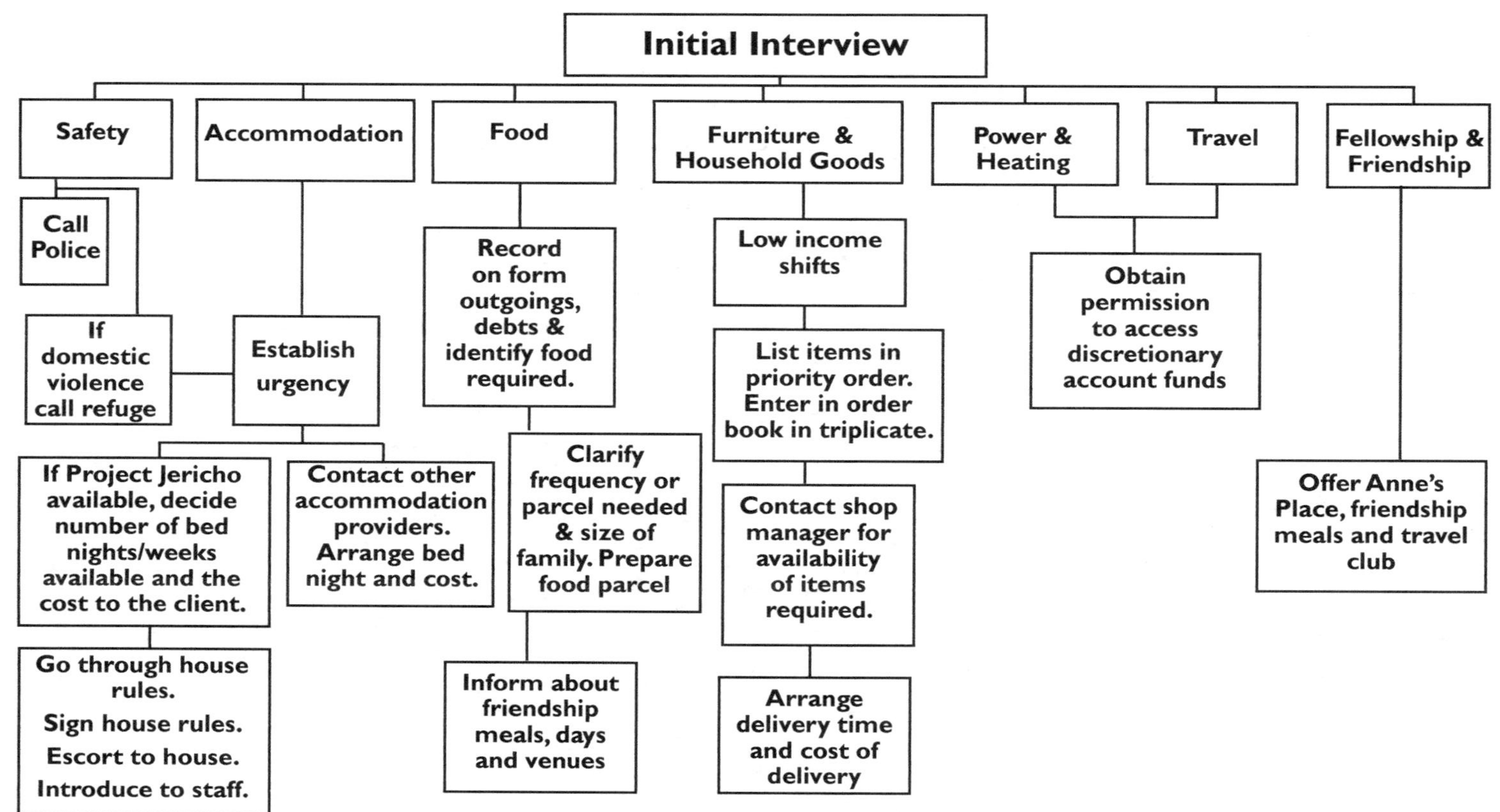

Initial Interview
Safety
Call Police
If domestic violence call refuge
Accommodation
Establish urgency
If Project Jericho available, decide number of bed nights/weeks available and the cost to the client.
Go through house rules. Sign house rules. Escort to house. Introduce to staff.
Contact other accommodation providers. Arrange bed night and cost.
Food
Record on form outgoings, debts & identify food required.
Clarify frequency or parcel needed & size of family. Prepare food parcel
Inform about friendship meals, days and venues
Furniture & Household Goods
Low income shifts
List items in priority order. Enter in order book in triplicate.
Contact shop manager for availability of items required.
Arrange delivery time and cost of delivery
Power & Heating
Obtain permission to access discretionary account funds
Travel
Fellowship & Friendship
Offer Anne's Place, friendship meals and travel club

Getting help at the Mission had been well established over the past decade. However, I was always amazed how a new person to Wanganui was directed to us, often with the encouragement that we could help.

Other historic services were to be discontinued. "Give-a-kid-a-grin" was set up by a previous City Missioner and had sponsored children from low income families to adventure camps twice a year – either with Green Pastures or YMCA.

Craft courses ran twice a month throughout the year but seemed to be best served through churches and community groups which also had craft groups running.

Lastly the weekly firewood service. Historically the City Missioner would arrive at the place the firewood was kept at a certain day and time, where people would fill their car boots with firewood.

Like many of the services the Mission offered, there seemed to be little rationale as to how we went about it. Some folk seemed able to get lots of help and resources, but others were not so lucky.

A new era had begun; the team, including staff and volunteers, was negotiating its way through management policies and procedures. These processes were developed then shared with other agencies so that it was known well what our core business was and how we went about it.

A founding member who visited said to me, "Change is something that we must embrace, and with taking a risk to do new things, comes change and with change comes high stress and letting go. This is all a very natural process." Wise words.

I was poised to make some difficult decisions about what parts of the Mission would continue and in what form and what would be left behind.

Chapter 7 — Core Services Continuing

Having made the tough choices about what services stayed and what went, and having them agreed by the board, I set about looking into services that would continue essentially as they had been for some years. These were: the community Christmas lunch, travel club, Anne's Place and the gardening team.

Community Christmas Lunch

I am not exactly sure when the Christmas lunch first started. It was often referred to as Christmas dinner, although it was served in the middle of the day. Like many cities there are people who struggle with Christmas and others who wanted to make Christmas a better time for these families and individuals.

When I attended the first Christmas lunch as City Missioner, I was amazed at the wonderful time people had. I saw the gift that it was, and ensured it continued during my time. Uncle Bill and Aunty Anne (as they were known) were the ones who created the spark and provided much of the labour required. Although they were getting older each year, it continued to be a success.

They enlisted support from their local marae to cook food and at the right time the food arrived and was served. The Christmas lunch was a feast to behold. A team of volunteers gave up their time to prepare the space, prepare and serve food, and clean up after.

Over the next years I found out exactly how much organisation went into this event. I began compiling information for this event: what needed to be done and when.

Planning for the Christmas lunch began in August with storing some of the donated catering tins and foodstuffs that were not really suitable for families. Gifts of food came from as far away as The Café at Waiouru and from Speirs Foods in Marton.

During November people began offering their services as volunteers, businesses donated food items, and others gave presents for needy children. In order to have some idea of how many people attended, numbered tickets went on sale at $2 per ticket, but it was never easy to know exactly how many people would be fed.

Food preparation and serving team

Next, I wrote up five rosters of tasks to be done starting with Christmas Eve. Each roster had a designated team leader. This first roster included the setting up of the space and the food preparation that could be done early.

The second roster was for food preparation, starting early Christmas morning.

The third roster was about meeting and greeting each person that came, seating them, serving them each course of the meal and ensuring they had enough to eat.

The fourth was the cleaning up, clearing away decorations and ensuring the hall was left clear and clean. A fifth roster was giving food to those who couldn't come to lunch or families we knew were facing hardship over this period. We would freeze any leftovers that could be stored for the foodbank. Finally, we packed away all the decorations and kitchenware that we owned ready for the next year.

Any frustrations of feeding up to 500 people were eclipsed by the smiles.

We were always grateful to the Council for the use of the Memorial Hall at no cost.

We moved from the Pioneer Room to the Memorial Hall during the time I was there because of greater numbers and the number of mobility scooters. Those with mobility scooters had to park in a line – parallel parking so to speak! Then they turned their seats to face the table. They took up much more room than the individual seats had.

We had entertainers, singers, dancers and music. Santa Claus arrived to give out presents that Birthright had given us for children who attended, and the atmosphere was filled with love, peace and joy.

By 3pm it was as if nothing had happened in the hall. Everything was away and cleaned, tired volunteers gave hugs all around for a big task well done.

Funding the community Christmas lunch was always a faith venture, "do the right thing and the money will come," I believed. In 2006 it all started early in the year, with the Embassy Theatre having a special showing of a movie and the Community Choir both fundraising for the lunch.

We were well ahead of proposed Christmas costs, especially as we had money left over from last year. By late November, as always, Christmas lunch tickets went on sale, and we took names of volunteers to help make that happen. Some of the volunteers were young children, some were grandparents, there were whole families; all had their own story to tell, of family overseas, that they lived alone, or that they wanted to show their children how other people lived.

Greeters and servers

A reporter and a photographer from the *Wanganui Chronicle* visited the Christmas lunch in 2006. Merania and Kirsty spent time wandering around inside and talked to some of the volunteers and people who came to the Christmas lunch. Afterwards I found them outside with tears in their eyes. They were overwhelmed at the need they had seen, and the wonderful service given by volunteers. Merania remembers how touched she was by what she had experienced and that I offered them a man's handkerchief for their tears. It was interesting to hear that from her as I went through a lot of men's handkerchiefs, they were good for tears, runny noses, cuts and grazes and I always carried two neatly folded in my pockets.

In 2008 I had my own special angel at the community Christmas lunch. He just walked in on Christmas morning and said, "I'd like to help this year" and after the last of the dishes were done and the floors cleaned, he said, "I'd like to come back next year."

We had several crises such as the hall freezer not working and the ice cream melting, but it was still a well-planned and executed meal. With military precision, 'Mr Angel' helped the meal happen, freeing me to enjoy the company. Thank you, Mr Angel, and to all the other angels who arrived as promised. You made the meal a lot of fun and created fellowship for many of our lonely folk, especially the pudding maker. As we shared our Christmas lunch it seemed that angels had gathered around us. The first lunch was served at 11.50am after grace.

We served 218 guests and 76 volunteers a lovely meal. The cleaning finished, and doors closed at 2.45pm.

The Christmas lunch of 2010 brought together a wonderful group of 110 volunteers aged from 7 years old to well into their 80s. They helped feed, entertain and wish Happy Christmas to around 400 people. I was always grateful to those volunteers who made it all possible and especially to the team leaders, some who returned for a second year in a row.

The amazing thing about the Christmas lunch was that we always began December without full funding, yet by the time it was over we had all the food, presents, help, and entertainment we needed for a wonderful Christmas for many who had no other alternative. Like the loaves and fishes story we always had some left over.

Mission Travel Club

From 2000 a Mission Travel Club (MTC) was trialled. This consisted of monthly bus trips on a cost only/no profit basis. The first trip was to be in October that year.

In 2004 the then chairperson, carried out a review and proposed to the board, "That the Mission Travel Club is the property of Christian Social Services and all monies belong to Christian Social Services." The board agreed and voted that the MTC be the property of CSSW.

There was no record of a funding application specifically for the MTC, either to subsidise trips or cover administration costs. The MTC, however, was included amongst the listing of CSSW activities. While some individual trips may have lost money, there always seemed to be a credit balance.

The MTC was made up of a fascinating group of people who were able to plan and fulfil budget trips away. Reports of fun and amazing experiences filtered through after each trip. The trips I heard about were to the Wairarapa, Manaia Country Hall of Fame, Te Papa in

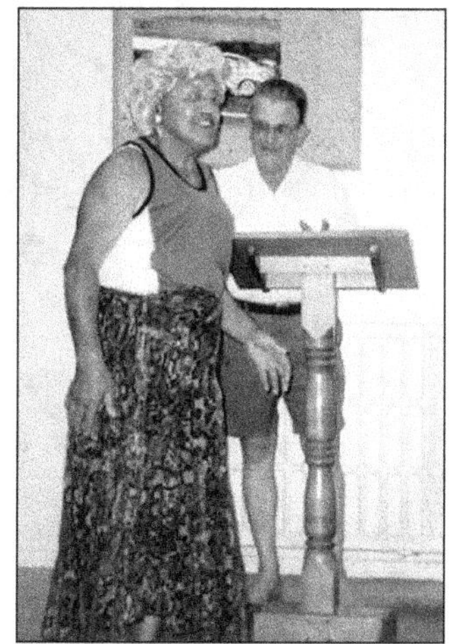

Bill Murray singing
"Ain't she Sweet"

Wellington, Palmerston North and seeing Clydesdales in Levin, all in 2004. In 2005 planned trips included Stratford, Foxton, Crosshills at Kimbolton, Palmerston North and a mystery trip to Woodville. In 2006, they visited Porirua Police College and Feilding.

Along with these were the yearly trips some distance away, held over a weekend. For example, a trip to Rotorua in 2004, and another to Papamoa in 2005, visiting kiwi fruit country and the Sunday Market. A highlight was Uncle Bill, dressed as a woman with a blond wig dancing to the music "Ain't She Sweet." There was a four day trip to Taupo in 2006 and there was much talk of the frivolity of a very successful holiday away. More than a holiday or a meal, it was about those people who might not have been able to finance or arrange a trip, holiday or a day away, being able to go in a group to new places.

In 2007, there were some changes within the MTC. At their AGM a new committee was elected and Bill Murray retired from the committee after many years. He was thanked for his long service with the club. Along with a new secretary/treasurer the committee put in place greater accountability of the MTC income, including raffles. This was a positive move forward.

MTC Midwinter Christmas Dinner

After meetings with the MTC executive, it was decided that trips would be a part of the Mission's core business and all its funds held in a separate account.

The new executive worked well and the first trip under their oversight was a visit to the Tawhiti Museum. They reported it was an enjoyable day and 35 members travelled. Some members were now pre-paying for the 2010 trip to the South Island, the "Top of the South" 9-day tour. However, the cost of fuel had taken its toll on trips and so the number of trips was reduced that year. A new bus company had been contracted and during the winter months they did local trips around the city, and had meals together, especially Midwinter Christmas lunch. I joined them when I could, but never did get to on an out of town or a long weekend trip.

Anne's Place

Anne's Place was described as follows in a summary from Anne Murray's point of view in the 2006 AGM Report:

> "Originally an outgrowth from the 'Soup Kitchen' in the old Christ Church hall, a drop-in centre grew as people continued to come even on those days when no meal was supplied. Anne had been called in to help with the Soup Kitchen, as it increased from one or two days to three days a week. She moved naturally from there to 'hosting' a drop-in/social group. With the impending demolition of the hall, the old Sunday School rooms at Trinity were rented and became the "Whare Manaaki" ('Friendship House'), in July 1993. With the foodbank and Office at Trinity, it was convenient for all. If there was a build-up of clients in the foyer, we sent them up to the Whare Manaaki for a cup of tea, while Anne or Bill were readily available if there was a problem where calling on a Kuia or Kaumatua could ease the situation.

> The inconvenience of being up a steep set of stairs and not being on a street frontage led to alternative premises being looked for. The site on the ground floor of Community House had plenty of pluses, especially as many clients were regulars at one or other of the groups based upstairs. It was named 'Anne's Place' in recognition of the vital role Anne had played over the years.

> They moved on 14 September 1998, officially opening on 5 October 1998. There have been few changes in staff, the volunteers remain for long periods with the centre. Many of them have been clients of CSSW themselves in the past."

Official Opening of Anne's Place

Anne's Place had a way of reinventing itself in new spaces, and that was to happen yet again while I was City Missioner. Through the seemingly unlimited energy of Anne Murray, with her husband Bill supporting her, along with a group of volunteers, Anne had continued to provide a place in town for those people who often found relationships or company difficult. Anne's Place offered a space to sit, always with a devotional beginning to the day, have a cuppa and a chat, make things, play board games or cards, and listen to music and entertainment.

Maria's Story

One of the first people to get the volunteer of the month award was Maria who had worked for the past seven years at Anne's Place, five hours a day, five days a week. She travelled into the city on a bus early each morning to volunteer. She could be seen leaving her home at around 6am to catch a bus into the city.

Her role was to clean and prepare the drop in centre for the people who would visit that day. She then spent the day serving those who popped in.

She was known for her quiet ways and was simply there for, and talked, to those who visited.

Maria getting her Certificate of Appreciation of her long service at Anne's Place from the City Missioner Shirley-Joy, with Maggie smiling alongside

She was always available for other Mission needs that came along and was quietly at the side of Aunty Anne, always helpful and freely gave to the work of the Mission.

Extending the opening hours in the afternoons and some evenings from 2006 brought other groups/activities that used the space and their donations contributed to the Council rent.

In June 2006 we were informed that the Council would increase the rent, and if we could not pay it then Anne's Place would have to move. By December the Council said that they had a paying tenant and Anne's Place had to move. However, by February 2007 it seemed that the Council no longer had another tenant and our tenancy continued.

A craft morning was enjoyed on a Tuesday morning. We explored the possibility of seeking funding to restart line dancing, as it was such an entertaining and lively addition to the drop in.

Anne's Place – Maria, Wendy, (unknown), Aunty Anne

Always looking for things to do, we helped get ready for the Christmas Parade by making crackers (the non-bang type) to give out to children. They had a small gift inside clean toilet roll inners wrapped with Christmas paper. The gift was a poem titled "What is Christmas?"

A time of worry and pain, like a thunder storm and rain.

Not being able to afford the Christmas gifts,
even 'merry Christmas' goodwill
makes the lights flash on the tills.

Just a little gift for this one – multiply it several times,
and the joy of giving suddenly fades away.

The "homemade gift," some say, "There's less cost that way,"
but for materials we must pay.

Nothing, maybe nothing, for all of us is the way to go.

Yet even in our homes we find a foe.
The TV churns out its wish list,
from Tonka toy to car, and all the things we'd like to have
are beamed in from afar.

Instead of love, the biggest word that's heard in this season,
is "NO," "We can't afford it," "That's the reason."

And arguments, persuasion, fits of anger follow on,
and whether we give in or not
dictates the next few months.

By Easter, maybe we'll catch up again and for so many
Christmas is a time of pain.

But what if it were different?

If all of us could train each other in giving priceless gifts
and change all that stress and pain.

A GIFT OF HOPE for future days
and LOVE to bring us closer.

A GIFT OF JOY and LAUGHTER
that will last the long years after.

A GIFT OF PEACE and HARMONY
so all can live together.

A GIFT OF LOVING FRIENDSHIP
that could last through stormy weather.

THESE ARE THE GIFTS THAT CHRISTMAS SHOULD
EMBRACE.

SJB. 2004

Thousands of crackers were ready by the time the parade came about.

More people continued to arrive daily, and it was a great atmosphere for some of our vulnerable clients. We were now looking for a new volunteer manager to share the load with Aunty Anne, as she needed time away to visit family overseas and generally take time off leaving the place in good hands. Trish, who worked in the furniture barn, became the fill-in manager with some support from Uncle Bill.

In October 2008 we received the letter from the Council raising the rent to $896.59 per month ($10,759.08 per year). Thankfully, we had an agreement of one months' notice, however the Council letter stated:

> "I must advise you that we have received an offer to rent the space at price recommended by the valuer we engaged. As a result of this I now give you formal notice of the termination of your tenancy effective from 13 November 2008. You do, of course, have the opportunity to have termination withdrawn if you are prepared to pay the rental, and operating expenses, that have been offered."
> *Signed by Graeme Paulger.*

We continued in negotiation with Council regarding their tenancy agreement which they would only offer us up to May 2009, as their tenancy of the building would be up for negotiation at that time. I struggled to see how they were willing to take on a new business in the space for only seven months. Our only funding for Anne's Place came from the District Health Board (DHB) and we were still waiting for a response from them.

We continued in the hope of getting sufficient funding to allow Anne's Place to continue. Despite this situation, Anne's Place continued to be a place of meeting and socialising and in August 2009, Aunty Anne and Uncle Bill celebrated their 60th Wedding Anniversary in the most appropriate place for them, Anne's Place, amongst family and friends.

Plan B was a move into a space at the Trinity Methodist Church, which would allow a place for people waiting for interviews or coping with children while waiting for food parcels etc. The lounge would give several benefits to the Mission as we often had people in our staff room for a cup of tea/coffee while they waited for us or were waiting for others.

This allowed closer supervision of the comings and goings of clients. The Trinity Methodist Church agreed to allow us to use the room and set it up as a lounge, provided we kept it clean and tidy along with the toilets and did not allow people to wander around the church complex.

The only time people would be free to go upstairs would be on Fridays when there was a Friendship Meal. There would be a cost to clients for cleaning materials and staffing, and the lounge could be open for the same hours as the Mission (8.30am – 2.30pm).

The closure of Anne's Place in October 2009 was an emotional time for many. Some 56 people gathered to say goodbye to the place they had called home for some years.

Anne's Place in Ridgeway had to be cleared of all furniture by the following Saturday and the power and phone disconnected. Anne and Bill set to creating a new space at the Catholic Church Marae.

Aunty Anne and Uncle Bill were an amazing couple who made a huge commitment to the Mission, whether it was on the Mission Board, working in the shop, supporting people at Anne's Place or on Travel Club Trips. Aunty Anne continued to be available to help others, sadly, Uncle Bill passed away in 2016. In April 2016 Aunty Anne was awarded the Queen's Service Medal and Laurel Stowell from the *Wanganui Chronicle* captured her beautifully when she wrote:

"Until Whanganui's Anne Murray got to Wellington to receive her Queen's Service Medal she was thinking it was all "a lot of rubbish."

Arriving at Government House on Tuesday the truth hit home.

"I didn't realise how important the whole thing was. It wasn't until I arrived and thought this is where the Queen and all those dignitary people come that it really hit me."

It was a beautiful occasion with a lot of laughs, she said. And there was another on Thursday in Whanganui – a morning tea in her honour at St Mary's church hall with about 60 people from her family, her church and her work.

Mrs Murray has kept open house at the church's Te Rau Oriwa Marae on Monday to Thursday mornings for the past six years. Before that she had a drop-in centre in Ridgway Street, called Anne's Place.

The centres have been open to anyone, from any walk in life, who is looking for a cuppa and some companionship.

"Those people out there, no matter what they do, they're still humans. You can't push them away – you want to – but that's not my way anyway," she said.

Speaking on Thursday, Catholic chaplain David Scoullar said Mrs Murray was an inspiration.

"Anne is the salt of the earth. We need more Annes, and we need more recognition for the Annes in our community."

Mrs Murray is 87, and said she planned to carry on her Marae Time mornings, with the help of sister Letia, as long as her health is okay.

She attributes her desire to help to her upbringing at Okahukura, near Taumarunui, and especially to her mother.

"I really didn't know my dad, because he passed on. We grew up with our mum, and the help of the whānau. My mum was the main one behind everything. She was gorgeous – a little wee tiny lady with a big heart."

In March 2018 Marae Time also closed. A newspaper article in the *Wanganui Chronicle* offered, "Rent rise and shortage of funds force shutdown of popular haven." Aunty Anne is quoted as saying, "It's hard to find another place for us to go, especially like this in the centre of town."

One of the special things about Aunty Anne was that she accepted everyone just as they were, she judged anyone. Mind you she did required a certain standard of behaviour and she got it.

(Photo used by permission of Wanganui Chronicle 29 March 2018)

Marae Time was a place for people of all ages regardless of who they were and what background they came from. Homeless people often spent time there for the fellowship and somewhere warm and friendly.

It was a place for the people who have the least has now gone.

The people are still here in our city, we see them from time to time if we wander down Victoria Avenue with eyes to see.

Our Space

This drop-in centre set up at the Methodist Church next door to the Mission Office and its foodbank had a slow start. A regular group of people popped in during the week and appreciated the quiet space. Most were happy to put in a koha. We often invited people waiting in the reception area, and especially those who seemed a little distressed, to join the volunteers there for a chat. It too closed as people in the church found having people there most days was not what they wanted.

Gardens

In the early days, the garden team was overseen by the City Missioner and there were stories of community service people going from garden to garden in a van. As I understood it the City Missioner had negotiated the use of about six private gardens that it used to provide vegetables. The gardens were tended by community service workers and supervised by Mission volunteers. Travelling between the gardens wasn't satisfactory, there was too much duplication of tools and gardening products, and it didn't really work.

Murray's Story

Murray Whitlock and Rosa Roach, along with another chap who worked on Fridays, were the gardeners when I became City Missioner. Although Rosa was in her 80s, her work in the gardens and her commitment as a volunteer was indisputable.

Murray would arrive on his bike at the Mission, sometimes quite early in the morning, with beautiful fresh vegetables in a box on the carrier, often barely contained in the box because the cauliflowers and cabbages were so big.

He told me when I interviewed him that he had started helping in the gardens in 2003 after retiring for the second time. He needed something to do. "I knocked on three doors – Wanganui East School, the local Playcentre and the City Mission – they all said yes. So, I started at all three. I was to help the gardener, went away for two weeks and then found I was the gardener!"

Two gardens provided vegetables for the foodbank and friendship meals. Another space was added at the old St Albans' site, until the section was sold.

One was a challenge, being down a steep bank and with three adjoining fence lines. We experienced vandalism and stuff getting pinched. The owner of the land later decided to garden the area themselves but had much the same problems.

Murray was like an energiser battery, he just kept going and going. Able to bring his own helpers and volunteers, I was always impressed by Murray's ability to go door knocking for the gardens. He picked up donated supplies in the mission van: poultry manure from Rasmussens, lime super phosphate and potash from Ravensdown, blood and bone from Wanganui Farm Supplies, plants from the Gonville Nursery.

The Mission paid for sprays and seed potatoes, and transport from time to time in the mission van, but he had everything organised and ran the gardens with precision. He told me that they have great gardens still going and that little has changed. He bikes around Whanganui with vegetables on his carrier, doing an unknown amount of distance, at least 6kms each time he heads out to the gardens.

Murray, Gardening Manager and his main volunteer.

Murray doesn't think many young people want to get involved with gardening these days as they are busy with other things. He does work with gardens in schools as he endeavours to share his knowledge with young people.

Murray is an unsung hero, who worked incredibly hard. Slowing him down at the food drive was a struggle, even when it was clear that he needed a break.

He had great drive, stamina and reliability. He contributed to leadership and work ethics. He often said,

> "Don't call yourself old, there is much still to do. Give me responsibilities (which I thrive on) and I will never miss a day. I still do the gardens, and I clean out the freezers in the foodbank,

because no-one else likes doing it. I quite enjoy going in and cleaning the freezers, and I like the people involvement. I find it quite enjoyable, fulfilling to a large degree. Keeps me active."

Volunteering kept him physically and mentally active and is good for his health. Nearing his 80th birthday, he looked pretty good and fit to me.

Determination sums up the wonderful people I have mentioned throughout this chapter; the Christmas lunch teams, travel club committee and helpers, Anne's Place and her faithful team, and the gardeners.

I reflected this in the City Missioner's Column on the 1st of November 2006, titled: *"Some people succeed because they are destined to, but most people succeed because they are determined to."*

"As I watch the volunteers here at the City Mission go about their work each day, I am impressed at how determined they are that the City Mission succeed. Success at the City Mission is about feeding people, listening to people, receiving and giving gifts, finding accommodation, always having the time to sit down and offer kind words. Don't get me wrong, this is not as easy as it seems. We are many people from many different walks of life, with wonderful moments of life experience. We see people when they are at their lowest often and try so hard to help them, sometimes we succeed and sometimes we cannot find an answer to their predicament. We are often abused by the very people we try to help. But we still try because we are a determined bunch.

Having stowed away the wonderful gifts of food you all gave, we are now preparing for the Community Christmas lunch. I used to get irritable with people who talked about Christmas weeks before it came, but now I am one of those who are counting down the weeks till Christmas Day; not for the gifts it will bring, like children do, but for the task of feeding up to 400 people at lunchtime.

I have questions on my mind, will we have enough food? Will the people enjoy the occasion? Will we have enough volunteers? I remember a saying from a long time ago, 'Curious people ask questions. Determined people find answers.' Arohanui."

Chapter 8 — Do the necessary…food first

The next four chapters are framed for me by this quote from Saint Francis of Assisi.

> I will start by doing what is necessary; then do what is possible; and suddenly I will be doing the impossible.

In the first column of 2006, I was thinking ahead to the daunting task of revamping existing services, the foodbank, Ezee Meals, friendship meals and bargain hunt/furniture bank.

> "Now on with 2006, our New Year's Resolutions made and already the year is under way. Like the wonderful colours at Kowhai Park, the New Year is sparkling and looking new. There is nothing like a new paint job, or a fresh look at some of the things in our lives.
>
> It takes courage to face our current reality. Often, we want to put a particular spin on things and pretend that they are somehow different to how other people around us see them. It isn't easy to look within and see our real selves, the self that we often hide from those around us, the self that is really only present when we come face to face with our own limitations. The danger is that we could lose sight of what is actually happening around us. We need a culture that is transparent about what is really happening around us. We need to take the risk of seeing ourselves as others see us. To try this out maybe these seven commandments might help: Thou shalt not pretend. Thou shalt not turn a blind eye. Thou shalt not exaggerate. Thou shalt not shoot the bearers of bad news. Thou shalt not hide behind the numbers. Thou shalt not ignore constructive criticism. Thou shalt not isolate thyself.
>
> We can't make progress in our lives while turning a blind eye to reality. We can face the truth regardless of how painful it might be. If you don't like what you see, change it! Catch you next week. Arohanui." *Missioner Column 4 January 2006*

The Mission's involvement in feeding people was well known around Wanganui through the churches and other agencies and was seen very much as an important service. Food has been provided in various forms since the 1980s, through the foodbank and the meals, before the Mission started; and through the sale of Ezee Meals from 1996.

Foodbank

The longest operating service of the Mission was the foodbank. Opened in the 1980s, it was situated in the old hall at Christ Church Anglican Church and was literally a walk-in cupboard.

Food recipients' details were kept in a note book, then as the demand got greater, an exercise book, followed by card files.

By 1990, due to cuts in benefits, the demand for food massively increased. Other churches and community groups were finding the same conversations began about reducing 'double dipping,' as people could turn up at any one or go around all the churches asking for food. Some people did this on Sunday morning when they knew the minister and church people would be busy with church and as they were often not intending to go to church, were given food, no questions asked to get them to leave. However, they would be back the next week, same time.

Often, church people didn't know how to handle this other than giving them food, or sometimes money for food. Unfortunately, money given may not have always gone on food, and then the giver felt frustrated and perhaps labelled people 'bludgers.' Hence the discussions about joining together to manage needs better.

Rotary Food Drive 2009
Food collected would be boxed and taken into the foodbank downstairs.

The Mission foodbank was seen by most as the logical agency to do this and encouraged the churches to bring their food donations to the Mission.

In 1991 a new site for the foodbank was opened at 40 Ridgeway Street. Getting enough food was always a difficulty and so in 1990, Mr Barry Pull, through Rotary South, organised and ran the first food drive. These annual food drives have continued and are well supported by Rotary Clubs and the Wanganui community. For some years they ran from the Memorial Hall and later from the Trinity Methodist Church Hall which was closer to the foodbank.

A foodbank manager was appointed, on a 9 month trial, around April 1993. By December that year opening hours were extended to 9am–1pm daily. In the years to come this was extended to 3pm.

The foodbank manager / co-ordinator/administrator was at the time a paid position, but like a lot of the work of the Mission, being able to keep them employed was dependent on funding.

Jill and a helper in the foodbank

All those who needed food were interviewed and their information recorded on a food parcel request form.

In these early days there were no real limits on accessing food parcels, but as time went on, it became important to get a greater understanding of clients' situations, in order to best encourage them to make changes, if changes were necessary to help them to manage their money better.

Later, this included a letter from WINZ if they were on a benefit, so as to ensure they were in fact getting their full entitlement. If there were difficulties with this and they were not getting their full entitlement, Gary Reid at the People's Centre was always ready and very able to assist. If they were struggling with managing their money, they were referred to the Budget Service.

One of my tasks as City Missioner was to ensure that the foodbank was working smoothly and any new guidelines that needed to be put in place were working. An identified challenge was when different people did the interview. We encouraged feedback from those wanting food and began to identify how different interviewers handled their requests.

When faced with demands for food, trying to tell the difference between the 'needy and the greedy' was never easy and sometimes saying "yes" was the easiest answer.

We were challenged, and sometimes left feeling numb, seeing people day after day with such great needs. To ensure that those requesting food were received without prejudice or judgement, a standardised interview form and questions to ask was developed. Parcels differed depending on numbers and ages identified on the interview sheet. Circular questioning allowed answers to be revisited.

We undertook a trial of foodbank clients to identify a list of the items and quantities they would need to feed them and or their family, for a given period of time. This helped them to plan their meals for the week and not simply depend on (or complain about) what we provided. This also allowed us to gather information about the most needed items and amounts used by different-sized families.

Another challenge was demands for money. I always had a policy of not giving out money. Food, emergency furniture, clothing, even petrol where someone needed emergency travel, but never money. This became a policy at the Mission. The board had historically put some money into a City Missioner's discretionary account to be used as the Missioner deemed necessary. The Missioner would purchase goods which were needed and then hand it to the client.

Sherylee's Story

Sherylee was a volunteer manager at the foodbank. It was a family affair with her children Terrilee and Caleb often helping. A group of volunteers came in each day and bagged the bulk foods we received.

They also sorted and shelved other items, taking time to identify the age of some products. We obtained date stamp information from the grocery chains to help us identify the contents of cans, and the use-by dates of cans without labels.

I often said that the two worst things around the Mission were old food and old gossip, both equally undesirable. We would often receive the left overs of someone's pantry, or some stores found tucked away at the back of the kitchen.

When I spoke to clubs I always took a box of such groceries. It contained items such as a glass jar of peanut butter with the statutory half inch of oil at the top, a packet of smelly fish things that looked like old whitebait becoming dust, an unused adult nappy, jellies valued at 25p, half empty packets of instant puddings carefully

Rick Surridge in the foodbank

rolled up inside and the top taped closed... These were examples of actual donations that people in our community had given to the Mission, expecting that recipients would appreciate them. The box was often received with great hilarity, which was then stifled by the reality of the situation.

Because information and statistic gathering was a bit haphazard, a computer program was used to record the information about people who applied for food parcels. This enabled us to see previous requests and what outcomes of interviews were.

By 2010 we had purchased a 'cloud programme' that all clients details of the Mission were recorded on. With this programme, once recorded, personal details were kept on a computer database offsite. Only non-identifying information was used for statistics gathering and fed back into the community, local and national government and to funders. Staff could access this from their computers for core services. Like all data it was only as good as those that loaded the information, but our dedicated staff entered this information for all core services. It was much easier to see all the needs of a particular client at once, regardless which core service they accessed.

Our statistics were now much more reliable, and the MSD hoped that these types of databases could be linked within community agencies. This was to get reliable information about which services/agencies were dealing with which clients and accurate statistics to enable funding to keep up with demands.

With a few changes and policies set, the foodbank continued to fulfil the growing demand, greatly helped by a caring community. This included those who would regularly drop in food each week, shops who gave bread and foodstuffs, and volunteers and staff who bagged bulk food, stacked shelves, cleaned and processed food parcels. Always at the frontline, the interviewers worked from 9am–3pm and often longer.

An interview could take quite a bit of time, as it was about creating a relationship with our clients so that they felt comfortable sharing with us what had happened that caused them to be in this situation. It was also about getting the full and accurate story. We heard many sad stories and some real hardships being endured.

These are some statistics from the foodbank:

	2007	**2008**	**2009**	**2010**
Food Parcels	1,084	1,246	1,657	1,384
First Time Parcels	185	72	155	304
Total Number fed	2,391	2,171	2,707	3,164
WINZ Standowns	38	40	104	164
Referral to Agencies	317	356	466	536

These statistics were drawn from the Annual General Meetings and *Whanganui Midweek* columns.

Ezee meals

In 1996 the Anglican Vestry was approached by Mission Foods in Wellington to act as an agent for their Ezee Meals. As they were not interested in doing this, they passed the information on to the Mission. The CSSW board entered into a three month trial in February 1997.

The first order took several months to go through. Order requirements meant that a number of cartons need to be ordered at once.

Ezee Meal clients were mainly aged and/or convalescent individuals. Home deliveries were made on Thursdays, with a minimum order of $20. A delivery fee of $3 was charged per order.

The Accident Compensation Commission (ACC) paid for meals for some clients (cheaper than paying for home-help to shop for ingredients and cook) and if ACC required a delivery other than Thursday, $6 was charged.

The range of main meals: meats with baked potato, mashed potato & two seasonal vegetables, 400–420gm, was sold for $6. Also 10 Light meals (four classed as 'All Day Breakfasts'). These were a different menu from main meals, with smaller servings of 300g, at $4.

Ten puddings, one a cheesecake to be defrosted, two designed for diabetics 180–220gm at $2.50. All except the cheesecake were able to be reheated in a normal or microwave oven, straight from the freezer.

Mission Foods organised at least one pamphlet drop a year, at their expense. All other advertising was through the City Missioner's speaking engagements and 'word of mouth.' Occasionally there was an opportunity to put a display on, such as the Disability May Day.

Mission Foods had supplied several freezers over the years as 'sweeteners' to price increases, etc, and one very large one when the Mission was required to order a minimum of 45 cartons.

Mission Foods raised their prices in November 2008 when the processing of the meals increased. The increased cost was not passed on to clients until 1st December 2009, when the cost of meals was increased $1.50 for meals, and $1 for puddings. Some of our regular elderly people had limited incomes and we felt that they needed time to adjust to the increase.

Friendship Meals

Friendship meals had been part of the Anglican Social Services for some time before the CSSW came into being. Called "Soup Kitchens," they were held on Mondays.

A meal was introduced on Wednesdays for people looking for a meal and social connection. They were often lonely and needed an opportunity to meet and eat with others. There was usually only soup and bread, and maybe a cup of tea, so these meals only met the most basic of needs. It was said the guests at lunch could tell who had made the soup by whether it was chunky or spiced! By 1993 there were three local churches offering meals and they were being referred to as "Friendship Centres."

The foodbank began to receive regular donations of frozen lamb legs and hoki fish. This enabled the cooks to 'branch out' and cook a full meal with vegetables from the mission gardens. By this time there were three meals a week and the aim was to get a meal each day from Monday to Friday.

Over the years different churches and locations were involved. With the new marae/hall complex at St Mary's Catholic Church and the re-building of the Christ Church Anglican's complex, there had been interruptions to how the meals were provided. The Central Baptist Church hosted a Wednesday lunch for some of that time. St Paul's Presbyterian Church was involved on Wednesdays, but initially their team supplied the meal from the Trinity Methodist Church's kitchen, before moving to their own site and then, sometime later, closing down.

By that time St Luke's Anglican Church at Castlecliff had started their own lunch, more or less independently. It was necessary to get another Wednesday meal in town and the St Luke's team gradually entered under the CSSW umbrella about nine years after the soup kitchens started.

The meals at All Saints Anglican Church in Wanganui East were a real co-operative effort, with initially five denominations supplying teams for each Thursday in the month.

Early Meals at Trinity Methodist Church Hall.
L to R Dixon, (unknown), (unknown), Tom, Leonie, Ron, Ann, (unknown),
(unknown). (Photographer unknown)

Later a church withdrew and that left four teams. Then the Thursday meal stopped for a time but was picked up again as it was seen as important, being the only one on the Eastside.

The question of how much of a Christian element was needed, and whether some kind of formal message should be involved in these meals had been an ongoing discussion. There was always grace said at the beginning of the meal (even at the original soup kitchens) with the occasional Bible reading when there was a special occasion. At a Tuesday meal at the Christ Church Anglican there was a 'God Spot' before each meal.

However, evangelising or proselytising was not encouraged. People came for fellowship, company and food.

Questions were also raised about cost and how meals were funded. There was a donation bowl at the door, but no pressure to make a donation was made.

When the meals became more than just bread and soup, and many people went around more than one meal a week, some people felt there should be a greater emphasis on 'clients' making a contribution.

Often donations came from businesses such as trays of bread from Cutelli's Bakery in Gonville. When the lamb stopped, the frozen hoki was still available. When both the bakery and the seafood company closed in the same year, it was said that CSSW lost "both its loaves and its fishes."

There were little niggles and matters that needed attention from time to time. As time went on a gold coin was expected, but some contributed, and some didn't so a decision was made that the meals were $2 for a meal of meat and three veg, bread, a cuppa and sometimes pudding. If someone was unable to afford that then they could go to the Mission and if really unable to pay, they would be given a complimentary ticket for meals. I was always amazed how the people who regularly turned up for the meals checked on each other, and any new people, to make sure they paid. With amazing budgeting by the meal team leaders and some money from the churches as well as the $2 per person per meal, the team leaders who did the meal planning and buying were able to include different meals.

It was established that the Mission would need to buy bread for the foodbank, and some of this would go to provide for friendship meals. There was a long debate over whether or not to buy meat for the meals. It was finally agreed that we would do so and Imlay was approached for a good deal. CSSW continued to buy sausages and mince costing around $3,000 per year. From time to time the larger supermarkets donated bread, produce, and items near expiry to the Mission. These often went to the friendship meals or the foodbank.

Friendship meals were all about providing an environment to meet and have a meal together, for those on fixed or low incomes and those who live alone so they could enjoy the company of others.

Some people liked to chat and talk about their day and week, others sat in silence, sometimes away from everyone, ate their meal and then slipped away back into the community.

We would sometimes notice that people met up at these meals and formed long-lasting friendships.

It was not always plain sailing at the meals. Often, I heard negative comments about the number of people who turned up in cars and were seen at five of the meals in a week, meaning they made these their main meal each day.

Sometimes personalities bubbled up, spilled over, and arguments happened. I would often be called in to try to settle the situation down. Some of the people who frequented the friendship meals could be very possessive and some did not like change. Some had their regular seats and if someone else sat there, trouble followed. Not unlike some churches I have been to.

The designated team leaders, whose responsibility it was to organise the meal preparation and serving and cleaning up, also became very good at diffusing tricky situations, enabling everyone to get on with their meal.

As City Missioner I would often attend meals, say grace and eat with those present. Many conversations about the things that bothered people would start at the meal and end up back in my office after lunch.

I remember someone from out of town being directed to a Friday meal at Trinity Church, who greatly appreciated the concept we had, and thought it should be shared, and that most towns could benefit from this kind of arrangement.

One of the difficulties I began to notice was that all the friendship meal team leaders and their volunteers were getting older, some of them in their 80s. Meeting regularly with the team leaders we began to put some framework around the running of these meals, the recipes and succession planning to bring in younger people.

In certain venues this was successful, but there was a strong resistance in other areas to younger ones taking over.

One of the gems I was to find out about from one of the team leaders, was a book called *Ministry to the Interior* prepared by a team of experienced cooks and resource people to assist with catering and cooking for large groups. Although somewhat out of date in terminology and, I imagine, some health and safety standards, it offered preparation of menus, quantities and ordering supplies, organising equipment, duties, plans for outdoor cooking and recipes for feeding the multitudes. All done with careful economy. This reminded me of my days cooking for camps for children up in the Kaimai ranges as part of the early work of Barnados. Sharing the information in this wee gem of a book was helpful to team leaders in varying their meals and trying some new recipes.

Some of the Christ Church Anglican Meal leadership.
Ann Tuhoro, Tom, (unknown), Dixon.

Each team had its own designated team leaders who chose their team, menus and helpers. At our meetings I encouraged them to invite younger people to come and join them.

In 2008 I was invited to attend the 10th Anniversary of the friendship meal at St Luke's Castlecliff and join Elsie (well into her 80s) who has been a part of the team for 10 years. A change of the team leader at Castlecliff came with ease and younger people stepped up willingly.

The Wanganui East meal had always been the responsibility of several churches taking week about, but they struggled with helpers from time to time.

St Mary's Catholic meal was under the able oversight of Aunty Anne and her team.

The Trinity Meals were under the leadership of Mr Dick Mansfield and his team, with new people joining from time to time. Dick was well into his 80s.

We were grateful for the meat from Imlay who had held their price for five years, but eventually that went up from $58 to $129 weekly. I checked to see if we would get a better deal elsewhere and we couldn't, so we continued with Imlay.

Meals continued to be available – Monday at St Joseph's Hall on Guyton Street; Tuesday at Christ Church's Hall, Wickstead Street; Wednesday at St Luke's Hall at Castlecliff; Thursday at All Saints Hall Wanganui East and on Friday at the Trinity Hall also in Wickstead Street.

Friendship meals were, and still are, a wonderful opportunity to rub shoulders and have a meal with some of the very unique, colourful and sometimes very different people in our community. The opportunity to share a meal is priceless.

Chapter 9 — Do the necessary clothing and furniture

Sharing was something that happened often between people and agencies in Wanganui. CSSW had space in the Birthright premises and several other sites for storing furniture; these were borrowed, and not rented, spaces. At one point the basement of Community House was used, and staff had to carry stuff down steep stairs with numerous twists and turns, an OSH nightmare.

I was told that in the past there had been some differences between Birthright's and CSSW's philosophies. Mission clients had no furniture at all, while others wanted to upgrade their furniture. A gradual separation followed leaving each organisation to do as they saw fit.

In 1992 when the Mission had its own van, the Furniture Barn got busier, and faster pickups and deliveries were possible. Originally items were only for giving away. Since there were large quantities of other goods building up, the Bargain Hunt/Garage Sale was introduced in March 1997. By May 1998 premises were rented in Drews Avenue. Once in its own space people knew it as the Bargain Hunt.

However, there was some abuse of the system, and both Bill Murray and the office administrator found themselves at the end of verbal abuse and demands. Some items gifted for needy families were found in second-hand shops or used as trade-ins at appliance stores. The system needed to be reviewed.

All items were priced, and clients encouraged to get WINZ quotes to pay for them where possible. Fire, flood and leaving a violent domestic situation were the main reasons for people receiving goods at no charge.

At some point it was noted that second-hand dealers were coming into the Bargain Hunt, so a decision was made that furniture was for community card holders only.

By the time I had settled into the role as City Missioner and looked at all core services (2004–2005), I became aware that there was an urgent need to restructure this service.

I visited the 'Op Shops' around the city, and I noticed there was now a focus on restoring old, rather than buying everything new. This was a trend I saw when I was overseas as well as in other centres round New Zealand. Retro was becoming vogue again.

I spent time talking with staff, getting a clear look at how the goods coming into the Bargain Hunt were processed. Noting that furniture, household goods and clothing were simply sorted, priced and sold, I felt there needed to be a process similar to shops enabling a stocktake to be done.

An inventory system was set up giving a paper trail from the pickup of furniture, household goods and those items dropped off by the public. We focussed mainly on bigger items, smaller items simply went out by the bag full or, in the case of toys, were given to children in the shop. The inventory also noted when goods were either given away in cases of emergency or sold.

This information helped us to assess how long furniture and household goods remained for sale, which furniture was needed, and which goods were slow sellers.

The Bargain Hunt and Garage Sale would not have been possible without the wonderful volunteers. People like Aunty Anne and Uncle Bill Murray donated vast amounts of time to this service. Others turned up maybe for one day a week and did whatever they were asked to do. But some were there each day.

With Uncle Bill planning to retire from the Barn in 2005, it seemed a good time to review how things were going and what needed to change. Synchronicity popped up again, and in this case, it was the arrival of a person to take over position of shop manager and to be a part of creating new avenues of work at the shop.

Mike and Sue

Mike came to help. Having run a small business, he brought with him skills in presentation and knowledge of the value of donated goods. Working with Mike, the decision was made to move from a two day a week Bargain Hunt, to opening more days during the week. It became known as the Furniture Bank.

Mike's team (L to R): Caleb, Rachel, Mike and Sue, George and Emma, George and Chris in the Revamped Furniture Bank.

In his role of Furniture Bank manager, Mike worked tirelessly in its rejuvenation. He balanced a difficult team embracing volunteers with experience, those who had little else to do with their time, and clients who were on Restorative Justice and Community Work sentences. Managing all of this and his own medical condition, he kept his cool most of the time and his sense of humour all the time! This was epitomised with his rendition of Frank Spencer which had staff in fits of laughter. He was our volunteer of the month of April 2006.

Unfortunately, Mike's health did not allow him to stay long. When he was planning to leave, a young man had come to Wanganui for a job which hadn't worked out. Wanting something to do to fill in time while he looked for work, he agreed to take over as a volunteer shop manager from Mike. This was my son Jared, and with his wife Lisa and their children, Jade and Jesse. They became part of the Mission family.

Several months later, in conversation with WINZ I was encouraged to apply for a Job Subsidy grant through a government funding initiative, for the shop manager position. Jared then became a paid manager of the Furniture Bank and helped develop the Mission Possible Shop.

Having paid staff meant that when things needed to be done, even though sometimes they didn't totally agree with it, they got it done. There had always been some difficulty with giving out emergency furniture. It had been left to each individual to make choices when the client was already at the shop and seeing things they wanted.

We developed a policy around emergency furniture, household goods and clothing. The items were only given out when at an interview, clients could prove they had no other avenue to borrow or pay for them. When we were contacted by other agencies, churches or emergency support groups, or Civil Defence we assisted where possible.

We had a priority order of goods:

- a bed for each person (doubles only for couples) one set of linen, blankets and a pillow for each bed

- fridge, kitchenware, table and chairs

- washing machine (for families only)

- drawers and couches/easy chairs were last on our list.

This meant that each family member had something to sit on, eat from, and sleep in, along with three sets of clothing depending on the season.

Clients needed a letter from WINZ if they were receiving a benefit or on a low fixed income. Clients had to be living independently, and not with family or others at the time of delivery, unless beds and bedding were needed. This policy was tested, reviewed, and then became permanent. This stopped the abuse, demands, challenges and manipulations from clients who thought they could go shopping and take what they chose.

The process was that a list was made by the interviewer, who checked with the furniture bank manager that the needed items were available, then a triplicate list was signed by the client.

When delivered, the client had to sign again to make sure it was the same person, and no furniture was left unless the person interviewed was present to receive the goods. If other agencies referred people to us this was the process. Everyone was now clear. Other agencies had their own processes.

George

Volunteer of the month George

Another of our volunteers was George. Gorgeous George as he was known, had been around the Mission Shop and other parts of the Mission for some years. He was always willing to help and often willing beyond his health capacity. Suffering from seizures, he was so willing that sometimes we had to say, "George, slow down."

He was a very helpful person both on the van and at the furniture bank. George often said that his own health improved with the regular work and how much he enjoyed being part of our team. George still helps around the community in many ways, the most visible is as a Frontiersman on car park duty at the many events we have here in Wanganui. He and his wife Lillian are often seen around town, a neat couple who in their own

Lilian and George Volunteer lunch

way have always served this community. He was our volunteer of the month of February 2006.

Trish and Maggie

Trish. Volunteer of the Month October 2005

Two special ladies, Margaret (Maggie) and Trish, had been helping around the Mission for some years. They helped the transition from Bargain Hunt to Furniture Bank to Mission Possible Shop. They saw many staff come and go.

Each day Trish would arrive with baking (I found out later, that her husband was a dab hand).

Maggie and Trish would arrive early in the morning and would simply work through the day, cleaning, sorting and preparing things for sale. They knew many people and always had time for a chat to those customers who came in.

Maggie and her grandchildren Terrilee and Caleb were involved in the Mission Shop. Maggie died in April 2013, aged 79 years. It was always said that she lived for the shop, and it was noted that she died only 16 months after leaving the shop when it temporarily closed down. Maggie and Trish were two of the many characters who worked

at the Mission and the Mission worked for them. The Mission Shop offered them an opportunity to serve in their community. They were paid $5 per day to help cover their expenses of getting to the Shop.

Maggie (Margaret)

Jill

Another story worthy of telling is that of 'stay-at-home' Mum, Jill. She had been made redundant and was not in such a good relationship with her children's father. Jill used to come shopping at the Furniture Bank.

She often found clothing at the Furniture Bank at prices she could afford. She was feeling a little bit lost and struggled with bills, a story all too familiar at the Mission and one I heard many times a day. She never had enough money and always seemed to have lots of debts. Her car was roadworthy but not registered or warranted, and she was getting lots of fines for the car and not able to pay them.

Like so many struggling people, she ended up commuting her fines to Community Service hours. She asked if she could do her hours at the Mission and then negotiated with the Probation Service to do her hours at the shop. Her tasks were to help out, sort, clean and arrange things so that they were tidy and looked good to sell. Straight after completing her Community Service, Jill applied to stay on as a volunteer.

I always enjoyed chatting with Jill at the shop and hearing her dreams. One was for a fashion parade to raise awareness of the Boutique. She thought of inviting young people from the schools to buy clothing and making them into fashion garments to display on a catwalk. Having the Universal Collage of Learning (UCOL) near the shop was great, as students often came in to buy things. We planned to have prizes for age categories. Unfortunately, it never eventuated. Jill was a tireless worker. However, she was feeling the pressure from WINZ to get paid work now her daughter was getting older. She was such a valuable volunteer and not one I wanted to lose. I worked toward getting a job subsidy for her too and employed her as the clothing boutique manager.

When talking to Jill about her time at the Shop she said,

> "I felt I could help volunteers in the same way the Mission had helped me. They would be embarrassed to start with, but they got to fit in. It was very much a family affair and I was able to have my children there. They were at school during the week, but when we

opened on a weekend I could bring my daughter Bailey in, and she enjoyed trying on all the clothes. She loved it and the other families there all worked in together."

Jill managed a number of volunteers and she was a good manager. Some of those people were doing their community service just as she had done. Jill got on with everyone, and nothing was too much trouble.

She said of the volunteers,

"I had a lot of volunteers and they were my responsibility, I loved most of them, Joan was there, she was a great worker and was there for a long time. Maggie and Trish were always there and working away, chatting to those that came in. Angeline, she did her community service and then stayed on. Quite a few people enjoyed being there and stayed on. I never had any problems with anyone."

Jill remembered going out in the van one time to a place out of town. This family was moving, and they had heaps of really good stuff. It was a wet day and there was a lot of mud on the road and driveway. Jared was driving, and he was great, but she really didn't think they were going to get back that day. She thought she wasn't going to survive this. She was so grateful when they got back onto tar sealed road again. "I decided, never again." Jill said it was a bit scary never knowing exactly where they were going on those pick-ups, or what the people would be like. She also couldn't believe that such good furniture was often donated to the shop.

I asked Jill, what she thought was most difficult for her while she was involved at the Mission? She said,

"It was the sad stories. I got to hear about their personal journey and how they were doing. This was the hardest and trying to help them out. There were so many people having hard times. We got some stroppy people, they had been to the office and were sent to us for clothing and furniture. They wanted heaps and all the best stuff. They would be trying to take stuff, without us guiding them. It was good to have a process and policies around what we could give as this made it easy for us to say these are the rules for everybody. I'm not saying it has anything to do with who you are or what you are doing, this is the same for everyone. I felt that we always had the backup of the shop manager, and if that failed, the City Missioner."

Jill especially appreciated how the Mission was like one big family and how people took an interest in her daughter Bailey, even though she could be difficult sometimes.

Part of the processes and policy work I did as City Missioner enabled us to have clear role descriptions for all volunteers, Police checks and attention to workplace safety. Jill found the volunteer role description useful as it helped her to know what was expected of her and not whatever others in the shop told her. We met some very desperate and lonely people, when they came in to apply for furniture.

Nourelle's Story

Nourelle came to the Mission because she needed a couch as hers was broken. Delivering the couch saw us become involved in a very desperate situation. Nourelle was dying.

This young woman had come to the Mission for help. Ravaged by years of drug use, she was becoming more and more aware that her body was nearing its end.

Our journey with her in her last year was incredibly memorable, probably in some people's eyes for all the wrong reasons. We visited her, we nursed her, we tried to help with her budget, we supported her family, where we could. She was such a beautiful soul, a fairy of a woman, with eyes which had seen much pain.

Many conversations about life, hopes, and dreams had been shared over coffee and she always enjoyed visits, whether it was me or one of the volunteers.

One memorable day, Ngareta was called to Nourelle's place by a nurse. Nourelle was very, very sick, and near to death, she needed hospital care immediately. Ngareta was encouraged by the nurse to take her straight away to Palmerston North hospital, as even waiting for the ambulance could be the difference between life and death. Ngareta called me and I immediately took the van over to Nourelle's home.

Throwing her mattress into the back of the van and gently lifting our precious Nourelle onto the mattress with the nurse's help, we headed for Palmerston North Hospital.

I drove using my best ambulance driving skills from some 10 years back, and Ngareta lay in the back with this frightened fragile woman, close to death. I angled my rear vision mirror, so I could watch and take instructions from Ngareta, who was as scared as I was that we would lose Nourelle during the journey. The scene that played out in the back of the van was one of devotion and care – a picture that would stay in my mind for years to come – a picture of an angel tending another angel, soon to be free of its mortal body. The afternoon sun and the whiteness of the back of the van somehow reflected the pure love in the back.

When we arrived, as the nurse promised, the staff at the hospital were there to meet us, and Nourelle was rushed into the emergency department, leaving Ngareta and I speechless, breathless, and with tears in our eyes as we waited the outcome.

Nourelle lived that day. She died some months later, and the experience of her in our lives will live on forever.

Ngareta and I reminisced about our experience and were especially mindful of it at Nourelle's funeral a year later, a time when she was surrounded by friends and family.

Hope and dreams, new beginnings, and making it through to a new day, were daily struggles for some of the more vulnerable people in our community. The Furniture Bank/Bargain Hunt was their place, a place to come and chat, buy something they could afford, look for a bargain to make their houses into homes filled with love and memories.

The things people bought from the Furniture Bank would often be made into colourful decorations around their walls and furniture. The clothes they selected helped their children feel OK among their friends. For people who bought their whole wardrobe from us, often dated in terms of the latest fashion, the clothes could easily be updated when a few bits and bobs were added. Then they could be as good as those they saw on the catwalk, Victoria Avenue being the catwalk of their lives, for many hours a week.

People coming into the Furniture Bank were noticing the spruce up and could see the movement from simply banking or holding furniture, household goods and clothing for emergencies, to becoming a retail shop.

Chapter 10 — Then the possible… Mission Possible Shop

As 2006 began, I was clear that the focus in the early months would be the Furniture Bank. Starting at the outside, in the driveway between the Furniture Bank and the building next door, there were always struggles with what was known by some as 'needle alley.' One of the least enjoyable and most dangerous jobs was cleaning up the alleyway. Yet every morning the staff and volunteers shovelled, scrubbed, disinfected, and cleaned it up. Later on, we put a gate at each end of the alley way paid for by the Mission. However, we never really did get the pigeon situation sorted. Between the pigeons and the 'down and outs,' there was always crap left in the driveway.

The Furniture Bank/Shop was growing, and this led to a conversation with the landlord to move some of our shop next door. This gained us a display window at the front and storage at the back, allowing space to check, repair and restore the second hand furniture and whiteware.

The new name sign written on the windows and the flag outside, heralded the move from Furniture Bank to Mission Possible Shop.

Now my focus was on vehicles. When people decided to give something, they expected it would be picked up straight away, so it was critical to pick up donations quickly.

The van transport was costly and often being misused. The grey van was in need of attention as it had been knocked and bumped about and needed servicing. I considered a new vehicle was needed.

Little was known about the history of the grey van. The previous City Missioner had first use of it, and it was available for transporting goods and people. When I tried to find a maintenance history, there didn't seem to be one. I decided to have it serviced and record all mileage in a log book. This would give me some information as to the usage of this vehicle, which areas of the Mission needed it the most, along with a clear picture of future needs for vehicles.

As the Shop got busier, this was very helpful. The van also serviced the needs of the foodbank, collecting food, delivering Ezee meals and collecting materials for the gardens.

It became obvious that with high mileage and required repairs, the van should be replaced sooner rather than later. For the work of the foodbank, Ezee meals, gardens etc., a van was ideal. With the seats in it was good for transporting people to appointments or meetings. For the Shop it would have been better to have a small truck with a lift on the back.

So, the compromise was to look for a van with a tow bar and have a large trailer for the furniture pick-ups and deliveries. As we had been supported by Wanganui Motors in the past, I met with Murray O'Hara and he found us the perfect van and had the tow bar fitted. The seating was removable and to protect the inside we purchased wood sheets and lined it to protect the paintwork, so that when needed, it could be returned to seating for around 10 people.

Now I had the task of seeking funding for a trailer. There were small grants available for this sort of project, and we were successful in an application to the Anglican Diocese. King's Trailers built the trailer to the maximum width allowable and as low to the ground as possible, allowing space for furniture to be carried on, via the back door, like a horse float.

The Mission had done little advertising regarding the areas we worked in, but now with core services confirmed by the board, the trailer would be a good way to advertise these. A big moving billboard. There was lots of room for sign-writing on the van and trailer, and businesses sponsored the cost of this.

Once sign written and out on the road, there seemed to be a renewal of interest in the Mission and it was seen all over the city. However, that also had its draw backs.

Some people took the opportunity to phone in and tell us where it was, what it was doing, just because they thought we should know. Maybe the driver had been spotted popping home for a break or taking something somewhere and seen by someone who thought they shouldn't be doing that. With no shed to put the van and trailer away off the street at night, the last thing I did most days was to drive the van and trailer to my home and back it inside the fence to meet insurance requirements that it not be left unattended on the street.

Not saying no to any donation often meant we collected things we couldn't sell. They had to be disposed of and the cost of disposing of them was high. We began to use everything we could, making goods out of bits and pieces, and repairing and painting furniture.

It was at this time that I was offered some clothing containers for the Mission from Wesley Social Services in Palmerston North. Big blue bins with a space in the front at the top to put clothes into.

We went and got these in the trailer and painted them bright yellow, sign written in big black lettering so that it was clear they belonged to the Mission. We negotiated places that we could put them and set up a schedule to clear them. This would be another role for the van.

Jill from the Clothing Boutique laughed when I interviewed her, and she remembered us getting the clothing bins. She would go with the van when they emptied them. "Emptying the clothing bins and finding dead cats. Sometimes it felt like Christmas, when we got things from the bins.

But some things were unpleasant, especially used sanitary stuff, used undies etc. Once they found someone sleeping in a bin." Jill giggled, "when I was young, I got into one once with my friend to get clothes."

In June 2007, the landlord informed us that he had plans to demolish the building we had the Furniture Barn in at 17 Drews Avenue. I had not considered this possibility. He offered the tenancy of the whole building next door (19 Drews Avenue) at an increased rental.

I had always dreamed of the Mission services all in one place, although I had not imagined it could happen so soon. I wondered if now was the right time? God often moved in strange ways, perhaps this was one of those times.

The move to 19 Drews Avenue would give us more space for storage and a bigger workshop. On the left hand side was space for the van and trailer, safely behind a roller door when not in use. It would also mean that the vehicles could unload inside. People often wandered into the workshop space and wanted things, even before they had been cleaned or repaired.

It was a workshop with machinery and we had restrictions on who could be in there. The shop front and clothing could be better displayed, and this would attract more customers. This building also had a second floor with a tenant.

Having a tenant above worked for a while, but it soon became clear that the tenant and friends did not just go in and out through the lower door but were rummaging through the shop all hours of the night and day. Staff were concerned about the stock going missing and doors being left unlocked.

At this time the landlord discussed the possibility of us using the second floor as part of the Mission Shop. Dreams were coming true. With extra space we might fit in the foodbank and Ezee Meals, and a proper reception area at the front of the shop. The landlord talked about putting in a kitchen, shower and offices, which could even include Anne's Place. All this with a graduated rental over 15 years. I was very excited.

There was no such thing as standing still at the Mission, for me or the staff and volunteers; there was always something happening, something new on the horizon, some change. It all sounded too good to be true.

The drawback of taking over the second floor was that the landlord asked us to deal with the tenant. It was actually the landlord's job, but as he was away from time to time and could not always to be relied upon. I wrote the appropriate letters with end dates and the landlord signed them.

When we finally got upstairs – what a mess. It was hard to imagine that a human being had lived up there. I remembered feeling sick to my stomach as we looked around. It was hard to dream a clothing floor rising up out of such squalor.

Jill was with me at the time. Downstairs we had often coped with leaks from upstairs, and now we knew why. The landlord was always going to fix the roof, but it didn't happen.

Jill vividly remembers the takeover of the first floor:

"When we moved upstairs to set up the Clothing Boutique it was a terrible mess. Someone had been living there and we got the task of cleaning up instead of paying rent, but it was really dirty.

Needles and drug stuff left there, rotten food in the fridge which had been turned off and benches with dirty dishes.

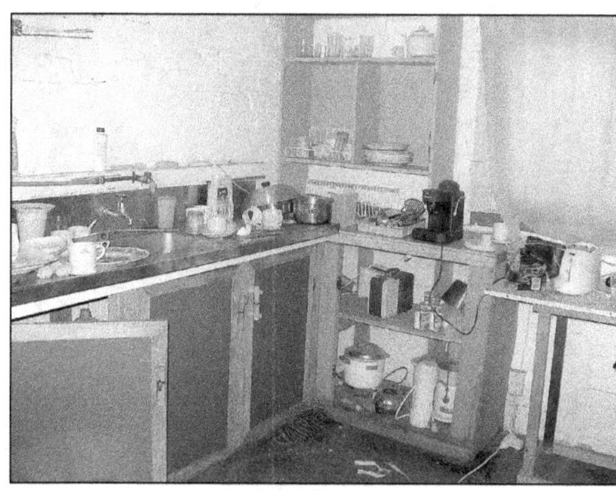

Before clean up

But we all mucked in and cleaned it up in no time, then set about our new boutique. This gave us another toilet, a shower and hot water for the first time. It was neat to be able to clean with hot water."

She set about designing and setting up the Clothing Boutique on the first floor of the new Mission Possible Shop. In one weekend with the team's help, she cleaned and moved the clothing and other goods into the bigger space upstairs.

Cleaning done

The clean-up team were amazing, they just got in and did the work. In just one weekend and we had shifted the clothing upstairs, made new racks and were open for business.

After setting up

On the clothing floor, she sorted, washed, repaired and ironed clothing. Before, volunteers had always taken the washing home and the Mission helped with power money and washing powder. Now we had a washing machine at the back, which ran most days.

Jill had lots of opportunity to focus on display and selling. She enjoyed the bigger area, with its better lighting. It was easier to clean, and the workshop team had built better clothing racks and shelving. We did have to manage leaks on wet days with buckets, someone once suggested some fish bowls with goldfish could catch the drips and look good.

As Jill put it,

> "We had much more space and storage, even with our $5 bags on Saturdays, which helped us move some of the clothing. However, most people took the best stuff, leaving other stuff only good for rags etc. I had regular customers from the UCOL who bought the better clothing. I definitely ran the boutique on a business line, and labelled stock with their prices."

In the three years Jill was with us she had moved from the bottom of one building, across the alley, setting up clothing racks on the bottom floor and then up to the first floor of the new building.

Jill said when I interviewed her, "It was more than just a job. I had a lot of fun." She talked of it being challenging yet rewarding work, and humbling when people shared with her their experiences and she felt she was able to offer practical help.

> "A lot of it was simply listening. It was always quite exciting as I never knew what I was going to face each day, we never knew what we were going to get brought in from the bins. Seriously, we had a good team, all the staff and volunteers. The Shop worked as a team, even though sometimes we hated what we had to do, but we kept it jolly. Some of the things we had to do were nightmares, but the friendships back at the shop made it all worthwhile."

Often staff and volunteers would resonate with these words from Jill:

> "Helping people and doing a good service, encouraging people to come back and spend their money or even browse around and be helped by having a chat. My life experience made me a better worker and more understanding. It was also a good distraction from what was going on in my life. Their journey sometimes made mine look much easier. There were often people much worse off than me and that made me feel grateful for what I had."

It was a sad day when Jill and her family left Wanganui to seek their future elsewhere.

Lisa moved from the Reception area at the foodbank to run the Boutique after Jill left.

This was now the Mission Possible Shop with clear policies and procedures. The Shop would collect donated items of clothing, furniture and household goods and as quickly as possible, prepare them for sale.

We always kept some furniture, household items and clothing for emergency needs.

Mission Possible Shop

If any staff wanted to purchase something they negotiated this with the shop manager. The stock was priced under the guidance of the shop manager along with those working in that area, always keeping in mind those people on fixed or low incomes. It was possible to put an item on hold, with a 10% deposit and five days to pay the balance.

This allowed those on benefits to get something they didn't quite have enough for in one week.

19 Drews Avenue

If payment was not made within five days, the item would be returned to stock for sale and the deposit forfeited. Goods were delivered for a small charge. WINZ quotes were given on stock available for sale and held. The shop manager was responsible for all security, health and safety requirements, and ran fire evacuation drills every few months.

Back of Shop

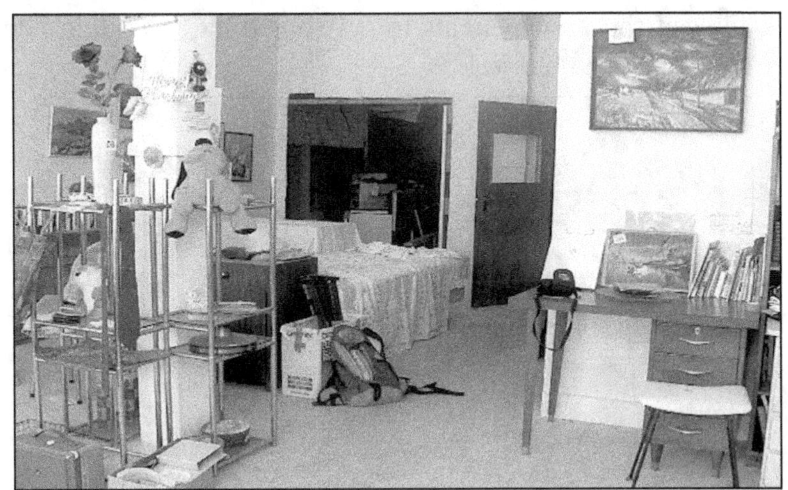

Shop Entry

We got involved in some unusual things at the Mission Possible Shop. One day I saw a request for use of a building to train dogs. Being a dog lover, I responded and asked what it was for. I found out that there was a dedicated group of people who were involved in search and rescue with their dogs. They needed somewhere to practice in a building with heaps of different things in it, with accompanying smells. Not many people were keen on having dogs running around in their buildings.

I agreed and spent a lovely day with the team and their dogs searching for firstly their toys hidden deep in the clothing and furniture, and then later finding children who had been instructed to hide and stay very quiet. It felt good doing this as I knew that there were times when we rely on these very dogs to find people, not only outside but also in buildings after earthquakes.

The next important area to sort out was the volunteer drivers. It was a demanding job, and most didn't stay long. Working between people who gave us things and those who wanted things was always like walking a tightrope. There were people who supported us, and other people who felt we created an unhealthy element in the city.

For many people, the van driver was the most frequently seen face of the Mission. They were often out on the road for long hours, trying to keep everyone happy.

I would say to the staff, "The two things that would challenge the Mission the most were bad food and gossip." We always had our fill of gossip. It was a shame that this was part of the history around the Mission – people talked, but seldom bothered to get the real story, preferring their made up one, usually a fairly dramatised version.

The board decided to employ a permanent driver, so long as I could find funding. If job search funding was successful, then we needed to be able to keep them on after that funding ran out. This was a pivotal role and the van driver was busy around the community transporting people, food and furniture. I knew that one driver in a vehicle ended up costing less in maintenance. With a new trailer especially made to take furniture and sign written with our core services, safe and careful driving became essential. We succeeded in securing funding for a paid driver. Ngareta was the first paid driver to manage the van team.

Having moved across the alleyway and settled into 19 Drews Avenue, everything was running smoothly.

People's lives were changed by coming to and working at the Mission. They often came to the Mission from a redundancy, illness (often mental illnesses like depression), family circumstances, from abusive families, lack of work or simply wishing to give back to others. Most found out that they were much more capable than they thought. They gained confidence and were comfortable giving direction to others, along with gaining new skills that helped them get jobs in the future. I was often approached to be a referee for volunteers and staff by future employees.

However, it was not to last, the dream had been too good to be true. I was glad we hadn't uplifted the foodbank and reception from under the Trinity Buildings. By late 2009 we had been told that we faced yet another shift and relocation costs. The building was to be taken over for the Sergeant Gallery, and we had to go.

Along with some board members, we spent weeks looking for another suitable building we could afford to rent. Finally, and fortunately we were able to find one around the corner on Taupo Quay. The team prepared to once again shift everything to the new space, also a two storied building in wrecked condition, but we were desperate.

Most of the shift to Taupo Quay was done voluntarily by shop staff and volunteers in their own time, over a weekend, to ensure the Shop could still operate during the week.

These moves were costly, money that the Mission didn't have. But such was the cost of progress to some in the city. We often felt that we were at the whim of the people in the city in more ways than one.

Always trying to do the best job we could for those that needed it the most, while encouraging people that had enough, to share a little of their good fortune by supporting the Mission in providing the basic necessities through our core services. At last with all the shifting behind us, the Mission Possible Shop could settle into doing what it did best, serving the community.

The Mission had a long history of being a provider of work for community service. The Mission Possible Shop had a very high number of community service people who completed their hours at the Mission. They were often the ones no-one else would risk having on their site. These are some comments expressed by Probation Officers, about Mission staff who had responsibility for orientation, training and supervision of community service:

> "Very approachable, has a good sense of humour, but still able to act professionally, dealt with situations in a capable manner, keeps good records and regular contact, manages conflict and deals professionally with those workers that did cause problems, and very able to work with people from all walks of life."

Another area that had grown was the number of requests to help shift people. We had always been willing to help families shift, especially now with the van and trailer. Requests came more and more from families who had found themselves having to find somewhere else to live. The reasons given were – failure to pay their rent, antisocial behaviour, mental health issues, and/or drug and alcohol addictions. They often put their heads in the sand about having to shift or put the issue into the too hard basket until it was very urgent and they were being evicted.

They were often people who didn't own a vehicle or had no friends that could help, people who had less and less discretionary spending and would shift frequently.

I felt it was very important to put a framework around this service to keep the van team safe, as it was they who went out to peoples' places and often faced very difficult circumstances. A low income shift policy was drafted in consultation with the shop team and trialled. It was then put before the board for ratification. This made clear what we would do and how these shifts would be carried out, including if any payment would be required.

Low income shifts were available to people on low or fixed incomes. We used the van and trailer to help them shift. These were clients who had no other avenue of help from family or friends, whose finances would not allow a professional shift.

Boutique Manager Lisa, Workshop Manager Jason and Shop Manager Jared.

They were encouraged to pay cash, apply for WINZ assistance or make arrangements to pay off the amount owed, if they could by regular weekly payments. Once interviewed, the shop manager went and assessed the number of belongings to be shifted, number of trips needed, and the number of staff needed to complete the shift. All belongings had to be packed and ready to be shifted on the day and time negotiated. No extra property would be accepted after this initial visit, nor extra trips or stops.

All property would be handled with care, and any breakages were the responsibility of the owner. No people, children or pets were transported by the Mission van. No rubbish was to be disposed of by the Mission. The client and/or owner of the property had to be present before any belongings were shifted, and if there was any dispute between landlords, tenants or other persons, the Mission team returned to base. There were few, if any, disputes once the policy was in place.

Other agencies also knew how we did these shifts, and often referred families who fitted our criteria.

As if the staff didn't have enough to do, the board decided in 2010 that we should be at the market each Saturday. Because the shop was already open on Saturday until 12pm and the shop staff were already working more hours than they were paid for, I offered to head this up and invited volunteers joined me.

So, every Friday just before the Shop was shut, we loaded up my mobile home and presented our goods at the market on Saturday from 6am. When finished we unloaded any unsold goods from the bus back into the shop just before it closed on the Saturday afternoon, so the goods were ready for the week ahead starting on Tuesday.

From talking with the staff who used to work at the Mission Possible Shop, it was clear they understood that the shop would never make a lot of money. Giving out emergency furniture, household goods and clothing ate into any profit.

Over the previous two years, the shop had grown from a furniture barn and garage sale, to the Mission Possible Shop; from a very part-time situation, to a full-time shop with retail presence. However, this had involved several partial and full location changes. At all times we remained focussed on keeping our prices affordable for low income families.

The staff, now settled at Taupo Quay, knew they had a good chance of running the Shop sustainably. Providing emergency furniture would always limit the available stock for sale, and limit profits made.

However, this was not how the board saw the future of the Mission Possible Shop. The board's thinking became clear by September 2010 when they advised the Shop staff that a key decision had been made. The board would make changes to the Mission Shop and seek a way to replace it (at some stage) with some alternative method, to sell the goods the Mission was given, but also to make a profit for the Mission from the Shop.

By December 2011, after months of gossip around the city, the board finally closed the shop and dismissed the staff and volunteers. To the staff and volunteers this seemed a foolish move as the cost of shifting and setting up had all been done and they felt it was full steam ahead.

But I guess all was not lost, the board opened the shop again in February 2012, under the leadership of spokesperson and board member Miles Bockett. An interesting story appeared in the *River City Press* on 9 February 2012, titled, *"Foodbank still running and Mission Possible to reopen under new name."* It read as follows:

> "…the Mission Possible Shop is to reopen this week under the new moniker 'City Mission Shop.' The shop will continue to be supervised as a furniture bank by CSSW and is welcoming donations and volunteer staff…the most important thing is to get the shop up and running again." Mr Bockett went on to say, "Having witnessed the surge of public demand since the shop reopened over the past month, public support has been massive. "Many people in Wanganui depend on it and I have even had people coming into my Ridgeway Street shop demanding to know when it would be reopened."

I found it interesting that in this write up, Mr Bockett acknowledged he ran 'Re-Dress' on Ridgeway Street. This was something I'd considered a conflict of interest for Mr Bockett as a board member, but it had never been addressed by the board.

That said, it was a sad ending for the staff and volunteers in December 2011. The staff and volunteers spoke of enjoying working together in an open an inviting space, that offered an atmosphere of hope.

They helped out, they helped up, and this was not limited to furniture and clothing but also helping people with personal difficulties. Staff and volunteers listened and offered a non-judgemental and empathetic ear to those who came into the shop. Nothing was too big that something couldn't change.

If someone had difficulties, someone else would step up and do something for them, there was always that cover, a hug, a hand on the shoulder, space to go and sit or shout or cry. The staff and volunteers often said to me, "It is a good place to work." The Mission Possible Shop had done its best in serving the Whanganui community.

Chapter 11 — And suddenly we will be doing the impossible…Total Care Budget

It was clear that putting time and energy into new services factored highly in feedback from the community, the Council and from discussions with other agencies.

When I became City Missioner in 2004, I was told there was a City Missioner's discretionary account that the board had originally set at $500. This was spent by the City Missioner and reported on at the monthly board meetings, and it would then be topped up to $500 again.

There were many times when people would ask or even beg me for money. My own personal preference was to give assistance in any way I could, but not money. It seemed that some of the people who came to the Mission knew from past experience that the City Missioner had access to money and were a little demanding. I would buy something for them, but never gave them money. Too many times I had seen good people give money for food, for the children, or clothing etc. only to see it spent on takeaway food, alcohol or drugs.

I often found it difficult to express to people who may have never faced that kind of life that giving money was not always helpful. It was hard for a person who always had a home to live in, with most of the things needed to enjoy daily life, to imagine what it would be like to not have those things. Some of these people had no house to live in, nor adequate furniture, nor anything to make a meal of in their house. They saw their children hungry.

I had experienced such times in my life and knew how deep the pain was, especially when you cannot provide for your children. The struggle I always had was to get people to understand what it was like. It is difficult for people without this experience to understand this type of pain and feeling of failure. I did not always succeed in this. I would often say, "Make your donation to the City Mission and we would make it go three times further as we knew the people and we knew the needs."

Total Care Budget (TCB)

The beginnings of TCB as we named it, are better told through the experience of one woman.

I arrived at work early in the morning, where people often joined me for breakfast or a cuppa. For some it was an opportunity to take medication with their food.

One Woman's Story

One morning, when I drove up, a woman was sitting outside the Mission door. She was crying and the moist tear tracks on her face and red puffed eyes suggested she had been crying for some time.

As we sat in the staff room she told me what was happening. She was a woman who had little in her life but had a regular routine around the city. As I was up early in the mornings, I would often see her around the streets. She told me her story of getting up in the early hours of the morning when most of us were sleeping, to be at the money machine shortly after midnight, when her benefit was paid to her bank account.

She would secretly withdraw her money and disappear back into the night. She told me that this was necessary to stop people forcing her to hand over her money. However, this morning some unscrupulous people found out this was happening and had stood over her until she gave them her money.

Now she did not have enough for food. She showed me the withdrawal slip and told me she had nowhere else to go. If she went to the police, she would be found by those who stood over her and she would be 'dealt to.' I provided her enough food for the week and took her home.

This was not the first time I had heard a story like this. I wondered what we could do to help. As I understood it, the Wanganui Budget Advisory Service gave advice only, and what seemed to be needed was a safe way to receive their money and ensure it went on the basics, rent, food power etc. There were others who were deep in debt and seemed to lack the discipline to do anything but spend it all straight away.

After talking with staff and other agencies around the city that also knew of these situations, and after discussions with the board, we decided to use the City Missioner's Discretionary Account to receive their benefits, pay their accounts (unless already paid out by WINZ) and give them the cash, often taking them to do their shopping safely. It was one answer to the constant dramas of people standing over vulnerable people and taking their money. Later the Mission provided a bank account to hold the money of some of our most vulnerable people. We also made this budgeting service available to those severely in debt and it enabled them to reduce the debt while managing better and learning new skills in money management through the relationship set up with the administration staff, who managed the income and expenditure.

The woman, who first took the risk of sharing with me what was going on for her and a number of others, died some months later from 'natural causes.'

She was loved by many and that showed in those who attended her funeral. Few knew of the fear and anguish behind some of her early mornings.

By 2006 we were able to pay client's accounts electronically and TCB became a part of the core services with clear policies and procedures.

TCB was offered to those special clients who had a known track record of indebtedness. At an interview it was established that they had little ability to keep themselves out of debt.

Added to this, their circumstances had been reported to the Mission by churches, businesses and other agencies within the city that they had approached for help on a regular basis.

A TCB Client needed to be willing to:

- disclose all debts

- agree to not increase debt unless agreed by CSSW budget person

- have all income paid into CSSW TCB account and

- show a commitment to be at the Mission at the time and day arranged to go through their budget and/or collect money for food etc.

To be on TCB the client needed to be willing to sign the City Missioner/ social worker as their agent at WINZ, or if employed, to arrange for a meeting of all three parties regarding their budget concerns.

That would be followed by arranging their pay to be credited to the Mission Discretionary Account.

Clients were also required to sign an agreement that would require all benefits, wages and allowances to be paid into the TCB account. It was clear that all accounts paid out of that account by the Mission would be from the client's income.

Authority would also need to be given in writing to the City Missioner/Social Worker, enabling contact with any creditors, and giving all details of amount owed, payment agreed to etc.

All of the client's income and expenditure was recorded and the information available to them each week or fortnight when they agreed to visit. A copy of this information was available within 24 hours, on request. It could also be sent to a third party if the client wished.

A seven day notice period (preferably in writing) was required to terminate their involvement with TCB, at which time all creditors and agencies would be informed, the clients' accounts finalised and an exit interview conducted.

An appointment time was arranged each week with clients of TCB to update their account and collect any cash required. If the client was given cash to purchase something themselves, they signed a receipt as proof that they had received that money and also agreed to produce the receipt of purchase.

TCB was really a last chance, and if they withdrew or terminated their contract with this service before they had completed their agreed term, they may not be accepted back on TBC in the future.

With greater indebtedness in the community, the numbers grew. We endeavoured to keep the numbers to under 10 families and individuals at any one time. But by 2008 we had risen above that.

It was a very challenging area of the Mission's work but had great results! Several families changed their attitude to budgeting and managed better on a low income.

It was often a frustrating task. I remember one person feeling trapped having overdrawn their account and been hit with $125 worth of bank fees in a week. That person became a client and signed up for help with their budget, through TCB. Others spoke of the new addiction, the numerous "cash and go" stores. These stores accept anything and give you cash. For example, if you pawned a Microwave for $40 cash, it would cost you $60 to get it back a week later. If you didn't pay the money to get it back within the arranged time frame they will sell it for its value, i.e. $160. We tried to educate our TCB clients about these establishments and help them avoid these pitfalls, along with keeping away from the clothing trucks that cruise our streets touting fashion clothes and goods – buy now pay later.

There were always more people wanting TCB than we could accommodate, and the only way forward was to have a team of volunteers or employ people dedicated to this work. We would rather have not needed it at all.

It was very rewarding when people on TCB succeeded in getting on top of their mountain of debt. I remember a client leaving TCB and sharing his experience with me. He said,

> "I would like to thank you so much for helping me through an extremely rough patch in my life, by taking the stress of the finances off me, and for all your love and support during these last few months. I feel I am now in a better place in my life."

It was for these people that TCB existed.

Another client had saved $900, where previously they could not manage from week to week, enough for them to purchase a car for their family of five, without getting into hire purchase or credit card debt.

I will leave the last words to Janice, our administrator, who took over TCB from me, allowing me to focus on Project Jericho. She reflected on her time at the Mission running TCB with these words,

> "Being at the City Mission lifted me out of my comfort zone and boy, oh boy that happened a lot of times. This helped me develop different skills which allowed me to help more people. I became involved with the TCB program learning the work from the City Missioner. All the staff followed the Missioner's vision. There were people in the community who couldn't manage their money and would always spend more than they had. As times were hard, more people were not managing. We worked with these people to understand how they got into debt, from drug or alcohol use

> or inability to manage their money. I have taken over TCB and it is good to see how people can progress, even when they owed thousands of dollars. Through TCB they could reduce their debt, sometimes by paying as little as $5 or $10 regularly. They get to a point when they take over their budget and continue to manage. I got a bit of a reputation of being a good person to come and see, but that I was quite tough too."

I remember one client saying to another while waiting in the reception for their meeting with Janice. "She'll help you with your bills, but she will tell you off too. Sort of like tough love."

It was tough love and we were teaching them something no-one had taught them before. Learning to manage our finances in order to have a roof over our heads, feed and clothe ourselves and our family is paramount to survival and happiness.

It wasn't impossible to get the budget situation sorted out, let's see if we can achieve that task of housing the homeless that has eluded the Mission since 1992.

Chapter 12 — And suddenly we will be doing the impossible... Emergency Housing

"There's no place like home

Ever wondered what it is like to have no home. Let me help you imagine. When the day comes to an end and you have no place to go, you begin by looking for a safe place where no-one can see you, away from lights and then you find some shelter or covering. You wiggle your body to get comfortable for a long night. You change position against the aches in your body, curling your toes and fingers, arms and legs in as far as you can, to help you keep your body heated. It is a restless sleep not knowing if you will be found or beaten during the night. What little possessions you have, are tightly secured in deep pockets or tied to your belt if you have one or stuffed down your socks. This is what living rough on the streets of our country is like.

Every week in our city there is such a person trying to sleep the night away. It is a long way from me in my warm bed, with a sheepskin underlay, clean sheets and a warm cuddly duvet. More and more here at the Mission we have enquiries for accommodation for homeless people. Thirty four such enquiries have come our way this year and the surprising thing about that is that over half of them involved women and men with children. I know for sure that other agencies have had people turn up at their place as well. It is time for us to provide a home for these people, where they can have a warm bed and hot food, with someone to talk with them and try to help them resolve their situation.

Next time you put your head down and draw up the covers of your bed, spare a thought for those living rough. You never know one day it might be you."

City Missioner's Column, Wanganui Midweek, 24 May 2006.

Emergency Housing

In 1992 the CSSW board strategic plan (bullet point 6) noted that there be, "no action on the decision on the Night Shelter/Transit Housing."

This, even though the historic information showed that from the beginning of the Mission in 1992, people had come to the Mission seeking accommodation – single men and women, couples and families and the Mission had arranged and paid for accommodation for them in other places. Fern Lodge, BSCP (86 Bignell Street), Castlecliff Holiday Park, Alwyn Court, Braemar and Bignell's Motor Camp were some of the places used.

Remember in 2004, I spent a night in Bignell's Motor Camp when we first visited Wanganui for a face-to-face meeting with the Wanganui Methodist Church.

We were very concerned about what was offered then in the name of five star accommodation. It seemed that others in the city had the same concerns. At the time of writing this book, I am delighted to hear that it is now under new ownership.

At one stage Rev David Day and the late Cecilia Boyd identified the need for a safe haven for young children and youth found in the city late at night, some of primary school age. They called a meeting with Mayor Poynter, Rosemary Hovey (Wanganui District Council), Marlene Wetton (YAC), The Manager of CYFS, Peter Gray (Police), Gerry Gibbs (YMCA) and Gloria Allen (Tupoho Maatua Whangai Trust). I am not sure what happened after that meeting but the meeting had identified a need for a Junior Night Shelter.

In November 2002, the board sent a letter to Prisoners Aid & Rehabilitation Service (PARS) asking for support of an approach to Jill Pettis, MP, for full government assistance in the earliest possible establishment of an emergency housing facility for Wanganui. The letter suggested that initial detailed planning and costs had been completed and the need was for males initially, but eventually to include females.

> "From our own experience, as a City Mission with many areas of contact with itinerant members of society, there is continual need for short or medium stay accommodation for several, quite distinct

groups. These are people for whom there are no alternatives (other than some rather dubious options)."

In the CSSW 2002 strategic plan, there was a move away from a Male Night Shelter, acknowledging the need for emergency accommodation for more than just single men.

Yet again, in 2003, there were several more attempts to kick start emergency housing. A letter was sent by Rev David Day to Paula Comerford, the Manager of Housing New Zealand, of the Housing Innovation Fund, in which he wrote of a "Housing Project" which PARS and CSSW had been working on for emergency housing for males. This letter showed consultation had taken place between the Police, the Department of Social Welfare (DSW) and the Wanganui District Council and that Rev Day had passed this on to Jill Pettis and Tariana Turia, the two local members of parliament for comment and hopefully for government funding.

In April 2004 there was a recommendation to the board that they formally accept overnight accommodation as an important part of its core business.

Around June 2004, a further meeting was called for by Rev David Day to bring Gordon Smith of "Anglican Action" to support the establishment of "The House Project" which was being considered for Wanganui.

Knowing that the board had considered emergency housing many times over earlier years, I felt it was time to do something. I looked at available statistics, any research, and talked to people in the other agencies, to get the full picture of the need for emergency housing in Wanganui.

I began conversations about what they saw as important issues, remembering the original question I came to the City Missioner's Role with, "What did this community need the Mission to do, that no-one else was doing, that needed to be done?"

More and more people came to the Mission seeking this assistance, and it seemed most urgent to get some form of safe overnight accommodation.

I remember a period of two weeks, when ten people needed accommodation:

- a couple who arrived from the South Island to be with an ill father
- a young woman with medical difficulties who was living in her van
- two young women who were in difficulty in their existing accommodation
- a mother and two children evicted from their rented house
- a young man who needed space from his extended family, and
- a man with a long history of alcohol and medical problems needing to be checked on by medical social workers, for two nights after a coronary episode.

My research suggested that between 5–8 people each week needed some sort of emergency or temporary accommodation while they found a new direction and hopefully permanent housing.

This was one of those times I missed being able to have direct contact with the Mayor and the Council. I remembered how special that relationship was for Rev David Day. This venture into emergency housing was one that we needed to be working on with the Council, but the incumbent Mayor did not see it this way.

I was able to meet regularly with Rosemary Hovey in her role as Community Development Officer for the Wanganui District Council – and we worked on getting emergency accommodation up and running, until she was no longer in that position.

The Council became even more distant and I could only bring a written report to the new Community Development Officer and was not encouraged to attend the Community Development Meetings or say anything unless invited.

I sent a letter to most of the agencies in Wanganui. I asked them two questions. Firstly, did they believe that Wanganui needed emergency housing and secondly, did they believe that the Mission was the right agency to run it. I also invited them to comment on their knowledge and experience of homelessness in the city.

Forty-seven agencies responded with two very clear yes answers. Yes, Wanganui desperately needed emergency housing and yes, the

Mission was seen as the Agency to head this venture. Along with Social Indicators produced by the Council, this became the platform for me to work in earnest toward emergency accommodation in Wanganui. Having been on the streets in other cities and having attended three International conferences on ending homelessness, (where I gained valuable information on housing issues around the world), I believed I had a good understanding of what people needed, and the form Emergency Housing could take here in Wanganui.

I had spoken with the people who had sought help from the Mission when they had nowhere to live, and one of the things that became clear was that in order to get a benefit sorted, an address was necessary. But what if you really lived along the river bank, or in the sand hills behind the surf club at Castlecliff, or in the bushes by the Warehouse and the many other places I knew people lived?

What if you couch surfed amongst your teenage friend's family's homes? What if you were not safe at home? And what if you had been in the refuge and couldn't stay there any longer, but still didn't have a house to go to? Each of these examples were from the stories I heard at the Mission.

Being committed to housing the homeless in our city, I recommended to the board, that they, formally accept overnight emergency accommodation as an important part of its (CSSW) core business. My recommendation was accepted.

In September 2005, it became known that the Refuge was being wound up and a new interim governance group would be restructuring the refuge.

A proposal was made that the Mission run the Wanganui Refuge over the three months covering Christmas 2005, with a possibility of an extension until February 2006.

This was a good opportunity for the Mission, to trial run emergency accommodation. With the board's approval I agreed to head up management of this trial, as the other core services seemed to be flowing well and the Christmas lunch was all planned.

The first house guest took up residence at 4.30pm the very day that we blessed the house and reopened for business. Another woman stayed for two nights and a family of a mother and two children under five, stayed for several weeks. We were mindful to take the most vulnerable over this time and to keep faith with the Refuge Interim Governance Group.

This was only a temporary arrangement and we did not advertise this accommodation beyond a few select agencies. When the National Refuge Collective was ready to resume the running of the Refuge, they thanked us for our work through last year and the beginning of this year and began rebuilding their new structure and committee.

The dream of a Jericho Inn went something like this – a house, possibly three or four bedrooms, with a live-in caretaker, open at 4pm in the afternoon, offering a light meal, a warm environment, clean bed, shower and breakfast in the morning. During this time, we could offer help to find more permanent accommodation or link people with the appropriate agency in the city that could best help them.

This idea came from the "Parable of the Good Samaritan" in the Bible (Luke 10:30–35).

> 30 Jesus replied, "A man was going down from Jerusalem to Jericho, and he encountered robbers, who stripped him of his clothes [and belongings], beat him, and went their way [unconcerned], leaving him half dead. 31 Now by coincidence a priest was going down that road, and when he saw him, he passed by on the other side. 32 Likewise a Levite also came down to the place and saw him and passed by on the other side [of the road]. 33 But a Samaritan [foreigner], who was travelling, came upon him; and when he saw him, he was deeply moved with compassion [for him], 34 and went to him and bandaged up his wounds, pouring oil and wine on them [to soothe and disinfect the injuries]; and he put him on his own pack-animal, and brought him to an inn and took care of him. 35 On the next day he took out two denarii [two days' wages] and gave them to the innkeeper, and said, 'Take care of him; and whatever more you spend, I will repay you when I return.'"

The public could be invited to be good Samaritans and pay the Inn Keeper – the Mission – for the accommodation and support needed.

Hence the name the Jericho Inn. Conversations with the Council and community groups continued.

An Emergency Housing Committee was set up in 2005.

This committee comprised of Dick Mansfield, Rosemary Hovey, Glen Horricks and I, with the support and knowledge of Denis McGowan, of McGowan & Associates (who had given his time and expertise on matters of Council requirements and nature of the buildings repairs/ maintenance etc.).

The terms of reference were drawn up to look at a range of possibilities for the continuation of emergency housing now called Project Jericho. The emergency housing committee asked these questions:

- Do we continue to offer emergency accommodation beyond 28 February 2006?

- Do we rent or buy a house for this purpose?

- Do we run this as a small business and take other occupants and run/provide emergency accommodation on the side, or do we simply offer emergency overnight accommodation?

The answers to the first two questions were yes. The third question needed further discussion. It was clear that this was becoming the answer to a decision of CSSW early in the 1990s – emergency accommodation in Wanganui was getting closer.

Knowing we had the income from the sale of Russell House, the emergency housing committee considered a range of houses for Project Jericho to continue after the Refuge – with a price range $230,000–$520,000.

There were conversations around visitors being there at night and then leaving during the day, having a midday meal at the Friendship Meals. Ezee meals could be provided for unexpected arrivals who had not eaten, which was often the case.

Around February 2007, there was a dialogue about Ozanam Villa, as a possible joint venture to set up emergency housing, between the Ozanam Villa Trust and Christian Social Services, or maybe CSSW should purchase the Villa. But in April, when an injunction was placed on the house, the housing committee decided that this avenue was probably not going to proceed.

The pressure was on, the Mission had accommodated, one way or another, 26 Women, 22 Men, 7 Teenagers and 38 Children since September 2006. Added to this in 2007 was a number of people who were seeking accommodation after Council terminated their tenancies to develop a block of flats.

Then came one of those synchronistic moments – the need was clear, and the answer arrived. I had often worked with the staff of Housing Corp, now known as Housing New Zealand (HNZ) regarding getting people into rentals, which seemed to be decreasing while the need was growing greater every year.

It was in November 2007 that I had a meeting with HNZ and shared the vision. It was at this first meeting, that I heard some units they owned would be available as early as December for a trial of three months.

Project Jericho back yard and play area

Known as 15–23 Somme Parade, there were eight units all together, well fenced at the back and with small, fenced outdoor spaces in the front. We accepted the offer to rent three of the eight units as a trial. Two units were for emergency accommodation and one for an onsite caretaker.

The rush was on, agreements were signed, furniture, bedding and household goods sought from the Mission Possible Shop and a caretaker to find.

Project Jericho was launched on 17 December 2007 (note to self – never to do this just before Christmas again) and became an integral part of the core services of CSSW. It had taken at least 14 years for the Mission to finally provide enough accommodation for homeless people in the Wanganui district.

Our first client came into residence on 20 December 2007. We began to count bed nights, which was each time a person was in residence for the night.

By Sunday 27 March 2008 we had accommodated 123 bed nights. We had turned away 4 single males who did not meet the criteria and two families ex-refuge, as we were full.

With the good work of the caretaker and his vigilance there had been no problems that could not be dealt with in a quiet and timely manner.

Discussions continued with HNZ to take over the other five units from March 2008, and as part of this discussion we held a public meeting.

The meeting was held on Thursday 21 February 2008 and the Project, along with the rationale for location

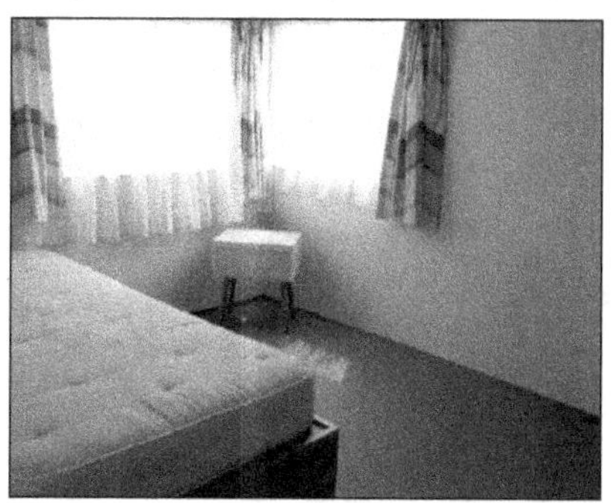

and the rules and staffing, were made public. To protect residents including our clients the location was not given or discussed by us.

Discussions followed, until we had exhausted all the questions. We knew that this was only the beginning of a long journey, and in the haste of setting up what was the trial period with three units for three months, we had not informed the neighbours, thus raising their suspicion right from the beginning.

As often happens, there were those who were not comfortable with the Mission offering emergency accommodation and certainly not in the place we were doing it. This is known as the NIMBY Principle. Emergency accommodation is a good idea, but 'not in my back yard.'

We were being watched and that was good, we needed to be sensitive to neighbours' concerns and yet firm when they called us regarding insignificant issues, often not related to our tenants.

Taking on the whole eight units to rent meant Project Jericho was a challenging venture. At the blessing of the new units there was just the right number of people present.

Some board members were in attendance, and also residents who opened their homes with pride to the visitors and had prepared the luncheon and cleaned up afterwards.

We were now offering up to 25 beds per night. The criterion was that emergency accommodation was offered to women and men, including those with children who were in need of a place to live while sorting out permanent accommodation. These people had nowhere else to go, no family or friends who could offer them a bed, nor enough money to pay for other accommodation in the city.

We were careful to interview people at the Mission Offices, so as not to raise expectation that they would be accepted, and also to try to keep the address as private as possible.

During the first 12 months of operation we accommodated an average of 12–15 people per night; single women, single men, couples and families with children. Their stays were from overnight to several months. Some of these people had chosen to live without the responsibility of a regular home, or were people who transited from other centres, or were evicted or unable to stay where they had been living.

The longer periods of accommodation were for families that endeavoured to get back on their feet because of drug/alcohol abuse, violent or abusive relationships or financial hardship.

Some guests had little or no belongings, while some had a whole house load of furniture. We accommodated both situations by removing our basic furnishings and household goods, thus helping the families manage for themselves and have their familiar things around for the children.

With several live-in staff, some basic rules of living together needed to be encouraged and often we found ourselves re-educating people on how to live with others in the community.

We worked with other agencies in the city who made referrals to our service and yet more agencies who helped in finding more permanent accommodation for our guests.

Those people who were able to pay, paid something for their accommodation. Those who genuinely had no money were helped by good Samaritans in Wanganui who, as the story suggested, offered a payment of a bed for the night and care for someone else, to us the Inn Keepers. If appropriate we let them know a little of the situation their donation helped without identifying information.

A social worker was involved as soon as possible to work through the needs of the client and/or links with other agencies who may already be involved or should be involved.

Long term planning was done, especially with regard to accommodation, along with other areas of the clients' lives that they believed were causing some difficulty. Once permanent or supported housing was accessed, other services of the Mission were offered, i.e. some were on TCB. Some needed food through the foodbank and/or emergency furniture, household goods or clothing through the Mission Possible Shop.

In July 2008, with the help of an employment grant, we were able to employ a live-in manager. Prior to this we had offered free accommodation to a manager who may have other commitments but was available at nights.

At the same time a management group began to meet weekly and worked on issues around communication with residents. Issues come with any grouping of people, especially those who have no choice but to live in emergency accommodation.

The management group was also able to keep in touch with neighbours, field concerns regarding residents, ensure fire drills and health and safety checks were done regularly. Workers from other agencies were welcome to attend if they also had clients in residence with us.

We signed a six month tenancy with HNZ, to be extended once the issues around monitoring were sorted out with MSD. We had a good turnout at regular resident's meetings.

Unfortunately, we had to trespass occupants from time to time, usually for abusive behaviour to another resident. With a paid manager and other staff who stepped up when extra numbers were needed, Project Jericho ran smoothly.

If someone needed a break from this highly stressful work, bearing in mind that most of the staff at this stage were volunteers, they only had to ask, or share this at supervision, and arrangements were made for some time out.

We continued to have around an 80% occupancy, with people in all the units, 435 bed nights in June 2008. We began to have a bit of movement with some longer staying residents moving on into their own rental homes and new people enquiring. Sometimes we had a waiting list.

One of the growing areas of need had been the numbers of teenagers (16-18 year olds) who required emergency accommodation. The number of teenagers housed shot up from 8 in 2006 to 48 by 2008. This led to raising with WINZ and HNZ the lack of places available for these teenagers. If this trend continued, we would need to look at a better solution than we currently had to accommodate these young people. From 2009 onwards, we endeavoured to keep the teenage numbers under 40 each year. In 2009 we accommodated 39 teenagers and in 2010, 36. Maybe that Junior Night Shelter, David Day and Cecilia Boyd identified, was the answer.

Toward the end of 2008 we began the CYF Audit process which would satisfy HNZ in terms of their request for monitoring of our service. We needed to contract the services of a professional to help us bring Project Jericho up to CYF Audit Standard which meant finding $5,000 funding. We were able to get a one off grant for this.

The number of people needing accommodation had remained high in October 2008, and we accommodated 577 bed nights.

There was a bit of movement around the units as we motivated those who thought that hanging around doing nothing was acceptable. We worked with the Mission Possible Shop to supervise them doing some work. Some residents enjoyed challenging the staff with a million ways to get out of doing anything.

Finding permanent housing was always a time for celebration, but it was difficult getting some single people into affordable accommodation, especially those people with mental health issues. They seemed to always slip through the cracks and were the majority of people needing emergency accommodation.

There were quiet and busy days and there was always plenty to be done around the property, mostly spring cleaning and maintenance. I often went down to check up on someone and found staff and residents working together on some tasks.

Staffing presented a problem, as the amount we could pay did not attract the best possible people to want to work there. However, with dedication and commitment, the staff ran an amazingly tight ship.

The next step was to have staff on site 24/7, beginning this discussion with the employment committee, and then the search for wage funding began.

A review of Project Jericho in 2009 suggested that there were still issues around some neighbours' concerns that, "the project is in the wrong place." However, being right in the city was helpful in terms of clients having easy access to all services and shops.

It was necessary to have access for service vehicles from the back of the property through a large locked gate, so we could not accommodate neighbours' concerns about traffic down their road.

There were concerns around families and individuals being together at the project. I struggled with this issue as it was no different to living in any street, except for the common use of a laundry.

The staff went to great lengths to ensure safety for all people on site.

At one time we had more families than normal, with families in four units and the two single units also full. Some of the residents enjoyed time working in the gardens with some board members, and the section looked great. There was always something going on at Project Jericho, usually a drama of one sort or another. Once there was a flood in a unit that meant that it was uninhabitable for a week to dry out.

As we came to the end of our second year of operation, a meeting was negotiated with HNZ for Friday 13 November. At the meeting the

HNZ Project Manager for the Manawatu/Taranaki/Wairarapa area was full of praise for the work that we were doing and the way that we kept the complex clean, tidy and well presented.

They discussed the possibility of supplying paint for the fences, work on the electrics, plumbing and other parts of the complex in need of maintenance. It was agreed that some of the fences were not needed and taking them down would improve security. HNZ would not agree to fence the gateway to Urquhart Street, but would consider a solid gate that was not so easy to climb.

We discussed lowering of the rent, but this needed to be discussed with the project manager's superior and she would get back to us.

The HNZ project manager contacted me later and asked me if she could introduce me to another trust she was working with that was having difficulty, operation-wise, with their emergency housing? Such was the esteem we were held in for the way we ran Project Jericho.

Some of their Stories

These stories represent only a few of the challenges the staff faced at Project Jericho. Some were funny, (usually after the fact), others were very serious.

One night, the male staff member on duty called me down to the project. He was quite concerned regarding a female resident. Our procedure was that no male staff member entered a woman's unit without another female staff member, so we went in together. Another procedure was that residents could not have other people stay overnight without staff permission. This was emergency housing and for safety reasons we needed to know who was on site at all times. It had been observed that this young lady had men coming into the unit just after dark and we needed to sort it out. We knocked and entered.

Each resident knew when they signed their agreement to be at the project knew that they were required to let us in when we asked. This would be if we had genuine concerns about any behaviour that was contrary to their agreement and could see them evicted.

We talked for a while and she reassured us that she had no one else there. We asked to look upstairs, and she agreed. As we entered the main bedroom we saw red rose petals all over the floor and a trail of them leading to the bed and scattered over the bed and a heart shaped pillow in the middle of the bed. Somewhat re-cheeked, I commented this was lovely, and was it for a friend. At that moment there was a bump in the double wardrobe, and I asked her if there was anyone else in the room. She said she was alone. I opened the door to see a naked young man with one hand covering his particulars and the other holding his shirt and jeans as he darted down the stairs and out of the building.

Some discussion followed downstairs and although we agreed that paying the rent was not easy, this was not the way to do it. She left a couple of days later, declaring the rent was too high and the profits too low. We reconsidered our interview process the next day to see how we missed this and saw her in need of emergency housing.

I was called to Project Jericho one evening, where one of the residents was in their room with a large hunting knife. I knew this resident had some struggles with life and was known to the mental health team.

It was always our policy with only one staff member on duty in the evenings that there was always someone else on call. This night was my turn. As a way of keeping costs down, I often attended such incidents.

I went with the staff member on duty to the unit.

Another known protocol was that if the situation could not be contained and resolved within an agreed period of time by staff then the Police were called. The signal for this was holding the hand up to the face in a signal to phone Police.

That night, a young man was in a fight with himself about coping with his thoughts of people coming to hurt him and of voices that scared him. His fears overtook his ability to calm himself and cope. Shut in his room with the knife he manifested this situation and it became critical. When I knocked and asked to enter the room, I was strengthened by knowing that the other staff member was just outside, along with several other residents, all ready to help.

His irritability continued to escalate, and I gave the signal to call the Police. On this night it was the Police's help that was needed for the safety of this man, and the other residents and staff. As a knife was involved, a number of Police came quickly, the young man was disarmed and taken away. It was not always this easy or quick.

One time we had to speak strongly to a young boy living in one of the units, who thought it great to climb a tree and pee onto the neighbour's property. It did not help the relationships with the neighbours but was often the sort of thing we needed to manage. A playground was just outside, but I guess this behaviour got him a better reaction.

Then there was the time we needed to clean out the garage at Project Jericho. We moved furniture around the units often to suit the number of people in the families, or individuals in a unit. It had got a bit untidy and needed cleaning out. It was great to see some of the residents come along and offer to help clean up.

This happened when we had the food drive, residents came up from Project Jericho and worked all that evening bringing in and stacking food alongside board members and students alike. They were often like a big family and we took care of each other.

I remember when one young man, a resident of Project Jericho, was very worried about Murray (the gardener) who always helped out on the food drive nights. This young man was so worried because Murray was perspiring profusely and very red in his face. The young man came up to me and asked if I could make Murray take a break as he was worried Murray might be having a heart attack. He was right on the button. Murray needed a break, something sweet and a cup of tea. We were used to Murray working hard and had not noticed how he looked.

Another incident with a person (who had only days before been released from mental health care) was when the staff member on duty found them walking around the back of the property, naked and fearful. After persuading them to come inside their unit, I spent hours sitting with them while they paced the sitting room, talking about things that made little sense. They kept looking out the window and threatening someone outside, even though there was no-one there. This was not easy because as they paced around the sitting room I tried not to look them in the eye so as not to seem threatening, but if I looked down, I would be accused of peering at their nakedness.

I always found those with mental health issues seemed to get much less speedy consideration, and in my mind, they needed more. Some three hours later, the person was escorted away by the police to the cells, where they were attended by the Mental Health Team. This was at a time when the Mental Health Team would only see people at the Police station, a safety measure I presume.

Once these kinds of situations were over, our first debrief would take place. We asked these questions. Could we have noticed something sooner? Did all our processes work as we needed them to? Could we have done anything differently for a better outcome? How was everyone feeling, now it was over?

A further debrief would take place at the weekly management meeting that all Project Jericho staff and volunteers attended, on the next Tuesday.

Unfortunately, episodes like this happened more frequently than any of us liked. We provided accommodation for people who could not find it anywhere else. Being on a busy road and near the river had its draw backs. Close proximity to the shops, government departments and services, Police Station and Hospital were benefits.

We were challenged by bizarre behaviour on more than one occasion and time and again put our lives on the line to care for them at the worst times of their lives.

Now for a cute story. We often had important people visit the project wanting to see how it ran. On this day we had two politicians visit. Grant Robertson and Phil Goff, who at that time was the Labour Party leader. They visited one of the families in residence and sat down for a cuppa and a chat. One of the boys in the family was home from school and playing on the carpet in the lounge. As his mother talked with Phil Goff, Grant Robertson seemed to nod off. The boy slid along to the Grant's knee, shook him and declared, quite loudly, that it was rude to sleep while his boss was talking. Out of the mouths of babes. Grant endeavoured to explain that they had got up early and done quite a bit of travel, but that didn't satisfy the boy, who strongly felt that Grant was being disrespectful. Maybe this young man had political aspirations.

When a resident left we invited them to do an exit interview and there were some very good comments from these. Here are some examples I remember:

> "I have appreciated the roof over my head and all the stuff that the City Mission have provided for me. I have made a new family and met people I will never forget."

> "Mean Māori Mean, thanks for having me."

> "I have appreciated the recuperation and respite."

> "The units were of a high standard of cleanliness."

> "Caretaker well suited to his work."

> "I appreciated the place to stay safe, sorry I am going to prison. I hope you will have room for me next month when I get out."

> "I appreciated the help and support I have received while staying on site."

I was always grateful for the dedication of the staff who went above and beyond their normal work. This raised for me the issue of responsible staffing of the Project and the mix of paid and voluntary staff. This was on a four days on (12 hour days), four days off roster including two day shifts and two night shifts.

There was a huge cost to having staff on site 24/7. The cost of this would have been around $130,000 in wages if all four were to be paid.

I believed in what we were doing and what I knew from my contacts around the Homelessness Coalition here and overseas that we were leaders in our management of Project Jericho.

These statistics were published in a report to the Annual General Meeting, and the *Wanganui Midweek* newspaper, and clearly showed the growing need for Emergency Housing. The total number of bed nights for 2010 was 5,797 and there were still three months to go until the end of 2011, with bed nights up to September 2011 at 5,376 already. Averaging per month based on 2010, a further 1,631 bed nights were expected suggesting a possible total for 2011 of 7,000.

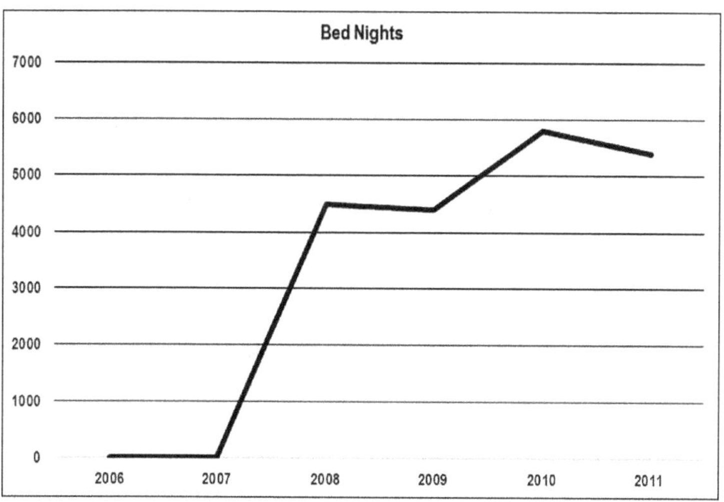

Mike

Before Mike came to the Mission he had gained some qualifications in the Alcohol and other Drug Service (AOD) field. He had assumed that this type of work would be easy to find. He told me, "I was impatient to do something I felt qualified to do. I wanted to get on with it. I was ready." In hindsight he realised that he was not as prepared as he thought he was.

Mike knew Hamish McDouall, the then Labour Party candidate in Wanganui, now Whanganui's Mayor. Mike was a Labour Party member himself and worked with Hamish on his campaign for the 2011 elections.

To start with the Project Jericho was just "a job." Mike had been out of work for six months and had come to Wanganui in September 2010 to do fruit picking and had delivered mail. When his wife was made redundant, he desperately needed work.

Mike reflected on his initial thoughts about the Mission and Project Jericho.

"I was interested in the work and how the mission was designed to work. The Mission was different from Wellington Downtown Ministries and Christchurch City Mission – in that it felt more caring… at this one there was a real desire to be hands on… It felt warmer. Project Jericho was different. Not a night shelter. PJ was caring and responsive, it was warm, homely… Within the units there was community… (the) impression from the people there was

> that… because of the way their lives had formed they gathered a little sphere around them."

He was only to be at the Mission for 22 months, just shy of two years, but he found it challenging. He said that:

> "In a lot of ways, it enhanced me as a person. It allowed me to grow in areas that were probably necessary. I learned a lot. It was very humbling as I had been in that position (homeless, destitute) for quite a lot of my life. I had been at rock bottom through drugs, alcohol, gambling, and found myself with nothing a lot of times in my life. I had slept on the street and it was not comfortable. I found myself able to help those people who had been where I had been… It was incredibly rewarding. On the other hand, it was incredibly challenging telling people NO, we can't help you, knowing for them there was nothing left. When we said we can't have you here tonight, knowing that the alternatives were not good for them… it was sometimes liberating saying it, but I never really enjoyed saying it."

Being a political chap, Mike found that the politics of the Mission management and governance was incredibly frustrating.

> "Especially when the City Missioner was removed from her ability to manage areas toward the end of my time at the Mission. The last few months were incredibly hard. I felt left with some very difficult decisions that I needed help with, but that help was not forthcoming. I had to make these decisions myself… but was aware I was flying by the seat of my pants most of the time. I did no harm."

However, there were memorable things that were not necessarily positive things.

> "The work with a young person over the course of a year, held some good and not so good times. It was good to see the change in him from when he arrived until he left. Kicking him out in an earlier time was probably the hardest part, evicting a 16 year old knowing they had nowhere to go was the most difficult thing I had to do. But taking him back in with his new attitude was memorable. I understand he is still doing OK, back living with his Dad. We hope things will work out for him this time.

> Also memorable were some of the short times with people, maybe only an interview. One example was when a client died as a result of

misadventure while intoxicated. This was tragic but not surprising, such was his lifestyle. Not everyone who wants to give up the negative things succeeds. I remembered it because I felt I may have made a mistake, although I am not sure where. I did not see him for a couple of days, maybe I should have kept in touch with him. It just sits oddly with me because I may have read him wrong. He was a really nice guy, who acknowledged his mistakes and yet seemed unable to change completely. I will carry this wondering for some time to come. This is outweighed by the many positive things we did with and for our clients."

Mike said, the most difficult things were,

"There was always an element of danger to the work. Some decisions could impact people's lives, for example, taking a knife off a drunk person. I had found a large hunting knife that was being used as a spotting tool and went to confiscate it. However, the owner of the knife took it from me and was drunkenly trying to show me how to use it. I was then left in a position of trying to take it back off this drunk and volatile individual.

Succeeding in this and getting the knife back speaks strongly of the relationship that was able to be formed between staff and residents. When we had concerns, we did unit searches and often found weapons in client's rooms. We never knew why they had them, and we were not always liked because we had to confiscate them. We had to be very good at managing conflict. The possibility of harm to staff was often present and yet those times of adrenaline rushes were also our opportunities to do our best work."

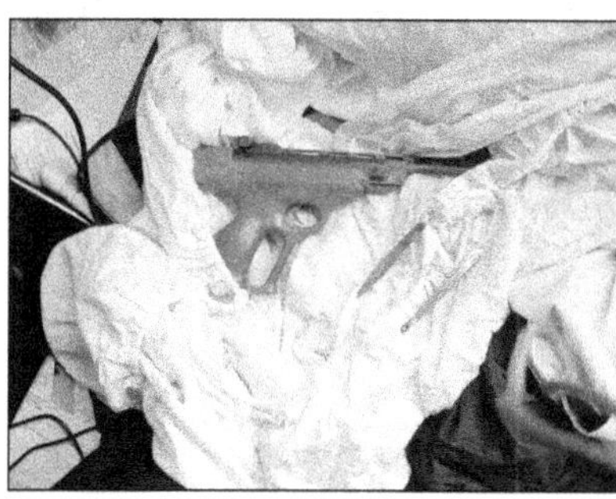

Mike said his experience overall was humbling, challenging, learning, rewarding, and enormously fun. He always saw himself working with clients, which would in turn benefit the Mission through positive outcomes.

Mike believed the community saw emergency housing as a means to help it feel safe and secure, that someone else was picking up the pieces. The community probably doesn't comprehend that keeping the vulnerable away from potential risk is a benefit. When people are desperate they do desperate things, helping to take that desperation away helps the community.

Mike believed that at a staff management level he was able to contribute to the Mission, especially PJ:

> "My personal learnings were that I was good at what I did, that I cared, that I will go out of my way to help somebody who needs it. That it's a little too comfortable for me to sometimes be the 'policeman,' that there are other ways to deal with a situation. I was learning to rationalise my own behaviour, before inflicting it on someone else. I asked myself often – How do my thoughts contribute to the way I am seeing something?"

I asked Mike 'in what way (if any) did being part of the Mission change your life?' He said,

> "If I look at my life before the Mission and now, I have more validation for the belief that anybody can get stuck and everybody needs help at sometimes in their life. The Mission was a great leveller, anyone can fall and may need to be picked up at some time – yet people can change."

Mike saw the Mission was an ever evolving beast, he knew that there would be always things to improve upon. The Missioner was always aware of those opportunities. He spoke of the potential for the Mission, and for PJ, and noticed when some internal challenges erupted.

> "When governance became management, there was a clash. PJ's potential grew further away, until such time as it was out of reach and unobtainable. This was sad, very sad."

Mike wanted others to know that Missions were often the last resort for people. The help at the end of the line. The Whanganui Mission strived to be more than that. Not only did it try to be the place of last resort, but also to tried to be a place that enabled people to climb out of the hole they were in as opposed to just catching them when they fell in. This was done individually for everyone and they understood that. It was personal.

From a personal perspective Mike said,

> "I was grateful for the people who allowed me to cross their path and also the ones who did not appreciate what I had to offer. For everybody that might have been pissed off with me there was still a place of respect between us. I don't think I pissed anybody off needlessly."

Frank Dillane, (a young man best known for his acting roles of Tom Riddle in *Harry Potter and the Half-Blood Prince*) is quoted as saying "Being homeless is like living in a post-apocalyptic world. You're on the outskirts of society."

My experience of being homeless did just that, excluded me from much of society and I would not wish it on anyone. I was pleased to be instrumental in Project Jericho Emergency and Temporary Residential Service and saddened to see it closed only a few months after I left the Mission.

My last contact with Project Jericho was after a call from Mike. The board ordered the closure of the Project and gave these most vulnerable people a letter and six days to find somewhere else to live. Mike knew that Project Jericho was often these peoples' last alternative and he was desperate to find somewhere for them.

One of these was Peter, who I spoke of in Chapter 5. Having lived in a unit at Project Jericho on and off for the past two years, there seemed nowhere else for him to go.

Some years earlier Peter had asked me to be his Enduring Power of Attorney (EPoA) should he not be able to make good choices. The team had cared for Peter as his health deteriorated, rolling his smokes, ensuring he remembered to eat and reminding him to dress for the weather, as his abilities to do these things and make good choices had declined.

Sadly, my next task was to get him assessed to be looked after as he could no long manage to live on his own. Left to his own devices, Peter, like the 'Blanket Man' in Wellington, could have been found dead on the street.

Instead, he lives in a community of people like him and still challenges people about his right to be treated well. He often contacts people in agencies around the city who were like family to him and still tries to contact politicians from time to time, although his speech is now difficult to understand.

Several times in 2012, other people contacted me and asked me to help them find somewhere to live. Once, when I was in the queue at WINZ, another time when I was out and about for coffee.

An agency called me as a last resort after they had done all they could. One young man who could not cope with more nights sleeping in the sand hills had simply wandered into the sea. He was so desperate. At our home in a warm bed and with some regular food, he appreciated a few days to sort himself out and then decided to go back to the South Island.

Another man had a job, but nowhere to live, so he lived in his car. After some years I still was being called as a last resort by people needing somewhere to live. I did the best I could, utilising the few contacts I had.

For years PARS has provided housing for those people leaving prison, without any fuss and very little funding.

I'm glad the Salvation Army supported by some government funding, is now running some emergency housing.

I found it frustrating that the lack of vision meant that we went around in a circle and had to start again, instead of having the faith to do what was needed the first time round.

Chapter 13 — A synchronistic orchestra of events

As 2009 began I knew there would be a change of chairperson and I had very much appreciated the last change of chairperson that seamlessly moved from one to the other.

The board (although challenged at times, as was I) had moved with faith and action, accepting changes to some core services and venturing into the new services.

I understood the challenge of and trust needed, to make decisions without sometimes actually meeting the people involved, for whom the decisions were being made.

The title of my column was *"Faith hears the inaudible, sees the invisible, believes the incredible and receives the impossible."* (adapted from a quote by St Francis of Assisi) This was clear in my mind as I watched new groups of people struggling with the downturn in the economy.

> "I was at the WINZ office today and watched the long line of people coming through the door. I thought our reception at the Mission was busy, but times are hard. Each day people seek help to manage their lives. For some it is as simple as someone to talk with them, for others there is need for a more hands-on approach. So many people are not able to pay their rent and are being evicted. Older folk worried about how they will manage with the interest rate dropping so low. Families worrying about how long they can keep their job and if the money can stretch far enough to go around all that they need to pay.

> How can the agencies in the city manage to meet the needs that are appearing before us? This raises for me a challenge. What will happen to all these people? How can we in this community, and at the Mission, manage? I believe that if we care about each other, we will manage, we will get by, together.

> Each day at the City Mission is a new experience; we never know exactly what will happen, who will come in to see us and what will they ask of us. However, we believe the incredible and in doing this, receive the impossible. Try it sometime if you have the courage, believe that something incredible can happen, and then be open to

receive the impossible. And if doubts overtake you…stop for a faith lift. Arohanui."

Wanganui Midweek, 4 February 2009.

I had experienced a great sense of synergy at the Mission. A time and place when we all worked together, and our joint results were greater than any of us could have done individually.

It was reminiscent of times before when I had shared in the strength of a team and now this team with its deep care for others and each member's capacity to touch the lives of those around them, was incredible.

This was a synchronistic orchestra of events and was the occurrence of encounters where there is a coming together like a large instrumental ensemble. A time when the lives and experiences of individuals are related to one another temporarily, and are conducted in various ways, where in other circumstances this might not have happened. There were coincidental occurrences coming together in a meaningful manner, with many unexpected benefits.

The Mission brought staff and volunteers from many walks of life, some who did the small things well, and some very able people who brought innovation and love to their roles in the core services of the Mission.

With clear role descriptions and management policies and procedures in place, Mission staff and volunteers were able to carry out the wonderful work they did with the least amount of direction and oversight from me. There was clear accountability for the work done, and there were high spirits.

In this place, where from one day to the next, there were few predictable things. The team moved with the distinct sway of Mission life. Sometimes gentle and regular, and sometimes with challenges that took us beyond our perceived abilities. Yet all things were possible, and everything that needed doing got done.

I was privileged to direct this synchronistic orchestra of people and events where the attitude of people spoke louder than their existence than their individual attitudes. We all linked with each other, with each person endeavouring to be open to and learn from others.

From 2004, for six years, the work of the Mission filled my waking hours along with some of my sleep and dreaming time too.

A normal day meant arriving at the Mission and unlocking the building. It wasn't unusual to find people waiting at the door for me. Jug on as a cuppa was always good with a chat. Then each one would be on their way. I knew lunch was available to them in the form of the friendship meals in the city and the surrounding areas and some church groups provided meals on the weekends.

By 9am the foodbank was open and people seeking food began arriving. Some stayed for a short time as they were expected and their food parcel was already prepared. For others, it might be a bit of a wait for an initial interview.

From the interview it was established which of our core services they would access and the procedure from there was clearly set down.

Safety was the first priority, then accommodation, followed by food, clothing, furniture and household goods. We also assisted with finding a way to pay urgent accounts for power and occasionally for travel costs. Sometimes it was simply important to have someone to talk to, to create a sense of fellowship.

Man falls in street

One time, Ngareta and I were travelling back from the shop in the van and we came across cars weaving across the road onto our side. Tooting and shouting at a person lying on the roadside of the curb with their head and body stretched almost across the other side of the road. Ngareta shouted, "I know him! Stop!" Ngareta jumped out of the van and I pulled across in front of him hazard lights on protecting him from the oncoming traffic. His body jolted and twisted around and Ngareta told me he was having a seizure. I got out and pulled several pillows from the back of the van and we knelt with him until the seizures had settled down. The swearing and shouting from people passing by him as we sat there was terrible. Things like "Shouldn't drink like that." "Bloody nuisance should be locked up." "So, this is what I pay my taxes for." Some people that passed by were so judgemental and I had to stop Ngareta from shouting back at them. Once the man could stand we gave him a ride back to the Mission for a cup of tea, and to make sure he had not hurt himself.

"All in a day's work for us," we said to each other and smiled. He was so grateful and promised us he would talk with his Doctor as these seizures were happening with greater frequency.

I tried to be in the office from early morning until about 1pm most days and kept outside events for the afternoons, e.g. meetings, paperwork, training, networking, speaking engagements and events for the afternoons.

For getting to meetings and speaking engagements I needed transport.

The Lada's Story

As City Missioner I had continued the tradition of using the van for all the running around, attending speaking engagements and visiting homes to assess people's needs. When the van was needed for other services I used my own vehicle.

In the staff room one morning, staff were talking about the van being so busy that juggling all the things we needed it for was becoming a problem. We needed another vehicle. I suggested we pray for one. The predominantly non-church going staff laughed but humoured me as we prayed for another vehicle.

Later that morning I received a call from an elderly man offering to donate to us a car. Not just any car, but a 1970 yellow Lada, in very good condition.

I understand our government did a swap at one stage butter for Lada vehicles and tractors. It stood proudly upon its original Russian tyres, needing only a little clean and tidy, and with a slight dent where the previous owner had caused it to kiss a fence post. It was ours if we wanted it.

I gratefully accepted the offer, as we never said no to a donation, and to my surprise I turned the key and the motor roared into life. We had prayed for and got another vehicle.

Not many staff wanted to use it though, as Ladas have

a Fiat gearbox setup. In fact, I think almost everyone hated the Lada except me. I have a history of driving anything with wheels and mostly quite fast.

Speaking of fast, I was heading to a funding meeting in New Plymouth one day, travelling along the longish straights between Hawera and New Plymouth, singing along as I often did and not paying attention to my speed, when I noticed a traffic officer go by in his marked car. I first checked my seat belt (having been a truck and bus driver I often forgot my seatbelt) and then straight away looked down at the speedo and saw I had been doing 120km. Now I know why he was looking at the Lada and then down at something in his car several times as he slowed and went by. I can only guess he did not see many Ladas go that fast. I was relieved he didn't turn around and I slowed to 100km per hour and minded my speed for the rest of the journey and back.

Having the Lada was great for me because most of the time the Lada was waiting outside when I needed it. One morning it appeared with a name on the side, "City Missioner's Limo."

The City Missioner's Limo worked hard, right up till the day it refused to go. It appeared decorated as a present, towed behind the new van at a Christmas parade and went on helping people in need. The Russian tyres lasted as long as the car did and after a short retirement as the emergency accommodation taxi it was sent to the scrap yard in the sky, well on Ridgeway Street anyway.

Some say it was in the local demolition derby. I think that was a fitting end, pity they didn't ask me to drive it. I shed a few tears the day the Lada died and then I was back to using my own vehicle as the board didn't feel we could afford another vehicle.

Sometimes I would call back into the office before going home to check if there was anything I needed to do. On one such occasion, I was met outside by two young women.

They called me "Mumsy"

They had been living in their car since coming to Wanganui and had not eaten for several days. Always believing that food was a great connector, I arranged a meal for them from the Ezee Meal list and we sat and discussed their situation. Their gratitude was accentuated by their smiles.

Accommodation was the next issue to sort out. After being in Project Jericho for a few nights we helped them into a flat and they received some emergency furniture. We helped get their benefits sorted and budgeting came next. By the end of two weeks, they were fed and housed, had benefits sorted and were back on their feet.

Many times after that I would hear a call "Mumsy" from up the street and there they were hand in hand heading towards me with big smiles.

The man-child

I remember fondly another young man, who visited me often in the early morning. A tall and strong 'man-child' with gang connections, living a simple life of travelling between centres.

One day I was coming down Guyton Street to the lights at Victoria Avenue intersection and there was a very loud shout, "Shirley-Joy." Being right by the lights, I looked up the street and there lumbering towards me was this young man, wearing gang tee shirt and black leather jacket proud with gang insignia.

Almost a complete picture, but on his bottom half, he only had on pink silk boxers, with red heart shaped patterns, followed by his long bare legs until they reached his laced up black army boots.

He quickly folded himself into the Lada and we headed to the Mission for a cuppa, then a trip to the shop, when it opened, for some jeans.

By 2006, we endeavoured to understand more of what happens in people's lives outside our office hours and how to help people change the way they do things, more than just giving out food. To help with this we began to be available '24/7' on-call.

Keeping a record of the after-hours calls gave us yet another picture of what was happening in the community.

Being available 24/7 was helpful and each of the paid staff members took turns in taking weekend and evening calls and recording them in a log book including what action was taken.

After Hours Calls numbered:
357 in 2006, 255 in 2007, 318 in 2008, 465 in 2009,
settling to 285 in 2010.

While there had been many interesting situations as a result of this, it was amazing how many people would ring Saturday or Sunday about something that could have been handled during the week – and which they would never dream of ringing another organisation about, during the weekend.

We then analysed the reasons people contacted us and found ways to limit the action from calls if it could wait until Monday. Some of these calls were genuine emergency calls. A number of them for people who were thinking about or planning suicide.

Jason has asked me to write the beginning of the story that led him to the Mission. He wanted it told, so that people might understand how much the Mission did for people at a time in their lives when they struggled with life and contemplated suicide.

I was unsure whether to include this subject as some professionals suggest that talking about suicide encourages people to contemplate doing it. I'm not convinced about that and have always been open about suicide, including my own attempts.

Jason's Story

Jason had come to a point in his life when he had given up on himself, his marriage and his beautiful little daughter Sarah. He had come to New Zealand from South Africa but had struggled with his life here.

Jason was referred to the Mission by mental health services after a suicide attempt that nearly left him dead and certainly left him with long term pain issues from an injury.

He found the Mission was a safe place to come and talk about what was going on in his life at the time. There was always someone there if he needed them. His life began to improve. He joined in with the work of the Mission as a volunteer. Thank you, Jason, for being willing to have your story told. The rest of Jason's story is in Chapter 14.

With our 24/7 services and support from the mental health service when needed, we were able to offer a wrap-around service helping people to find a place where they were safe, could heal and rebuild their lives.

Many people sought solace and help from the Mission at a time they considered ending their lives. They felt there was nothing left for them. They couldn't see a future and felt that they were holding their family and loved ones back by feeling sad and lost a lot of the time.

A Mental Health leaflet defines suicidal thoughts, or suicidal ideation, "as thoughts that can range from a detailed plan to a fleeting consideration." The leaflet goes on to say, "Most people who experience suicidal ideation do not carry it through, although some may make suicide attempts. Anyone who has suicidal thoughts should ask for help." Often when people called us they were asking for help.

Appreciation for Volunteers

With a team of amazing volunteers that often worked long hours who were called in for emergencies and cleaned up after others, I wanted to show my appreciation. With the board's permission in 2008 I planned a staff Christmas dinner at a local restaurant.

I printed certificates of voluntary service and had them ready for presentation. We gathered at the Lifferton Restaurant and with the sound of Christmas music staff, volunteers, and their families mixed with past and present board members.

It was a wonderful evening.

Now don't get me wrong, that doesn't mean that everyone got on really well with each other all the time, that was an impossibility –

but each team had a manager for each of the main core services, who knew well the nature of the work we did.

Each core service was to some degree scripted and yet open to change. That is, if the change was researched, specific and achievable. We walked in each other's shoes when needed with synchronicity infused around the whole of the Mission. This was at times both challenging and exciting. Things that happened more often than not worked out well.

Baby Jericho and his Mum

There had been the wonderful stories, like our own baby at the Mission. A young woman came to the city with her partner. They lived at Project Jericho for a while, but late in her pregnancy she and her two year old daughter came to live with Tony and me, where Jericho was born. We had a full house and family for over a year.

Jericho's Mum wanted to give something back to the Mission for the help we'd given her, and she became one of the volunteer receptionists. Watching her confidence grow was great as she became part of the team for a time.

Now we had a cohesive team including City Missioner, administrator, and managers for the foodbank, Mission Possible Shop, Clothing Boutique, Anne's Place and Project Jericho. At Project Jericho there were three other paid staff who along with the manager covered the emergency housing and 24/7 calls. Along with the faithful 100+ volunteers whose numbers remained static, although some retired and some moved away, and others offered their time to different agencies.

Baby Jericho

The role of administrator was a pivotal role to the smooth running of the Mission. Their support for me as City Missioner was integral, as was their secretarial support, ability

Jesse, Jericho and Jade

to understand and work with me on funding applications, maintain financial systems, interface with volunteers, members of the public and other community organisations. Another part of the job was to front the reception area.

The Administrators

These talented people followed in the able footsteps of the first receptionist. They each brought their uniqueness, their gifts and skills to the position.

The constant search for funding was a 365 day a year process. We searched for funding that fitted what we did, applied, and waited to see if we were successful. Later accounting for how these grants were spent.

The job of fundraising in itself was almost a full-time job. Although a governance responsibility, it had always been left to the City Missioner, something the previous City Missioner Rev David Day had lamented.

It meant raising up to $500,000 each year. Mostly we were successful with our applications as we always had the data and statistics to back them up.

Jill was already in the position of administrator when I was employed. At that time, it was a dual role of administrator/receptionist and was a big challenge that Jill did well.

Jill – administrator

Being available on the front counter with the constant interruptions of people coming in, trying to juggle funding applications, finances and ensuring the volunteers got their reimbursements meant full-on hours from about 9am–1pm or thereabouts. This was as well as being the secretary to the board. It was a stressful job.

It was one of the hardest and most demanding roles in the Mission. Unfortunately, Jill's health deteriorated, and we said our farewell to her.

It was such a big job and was high on my list for a review and possible change. In clarifying the role description, it was clear to me that this was two roles one of administration and another as a receptionist.

The roles were separated, and we were able to take on volunteers and students to train for the reception area, answering the phone, processing people on to interviews, selling Ezee Meals and directing clients to the person they needed to see. By the time I left several young women had worked voluntarily for us after leaving school, got some skills doing the receptionist role and then found full-time work.

Kerri arrived and brought good clear thinking and skills enabling her to easily fit into the role along with experience in running businesses and Refuge work. Her social work skills were helpful, even covering for me at a time I needed to be away.

Volunteer receptionist Lisa, Administrator Kerri
and a foodbank volunteer in the staff room.

Moana followed after Kerri left. In 2008 we were a bit late getting the Christmas income and expenditure together. This was because Moana was due to have her baby around 9 February.

Not quite as planned, the beautiful baby girl arrived on 18 January, a water birth at 6am, then at 9am they headed home via McDonalds. We were delighted for Moana and Dave. Moana stayed on for a while with her baby sleeping in the store room or the office. Us ladies got a bit 'clucky.'

Reception

Then Rosemary became a part of our team, she quickly picked up the role and had an eye for streamlining our systems. Rosemary was experienced in fund raising which was helpful as we sensed that the future of funding non-government agencies may lie with the ever growing power of the MSD, so it was good for Rosemary and I to attend their Contractors Services Forum.

Janice's Story

Next Janice joined us as Administrator. At first, I wondered if an older person could cope with the challenges of the Mission. I should never have doubted. She did. Janice took everything in her stride, most probably because of her background in the Salvation Army.

She told me when I interviewed her that,

> "As a committed Christian I felt that we are here on this earth
> to help each other and there are lots of people who through an
> organisation like the Mission, I could channel my energy to help,
> something to put my Christian beliefs into practice."

Janice had a gentle yet a no nonsense way of caring for people who behaved somewhat differently to her. With a sound background in hospital administration, supporting herself, she claimed the job when she saw it advertised. She didn't get the job first time around and was quite deflated, but thought, "...one door closes and another opens." She decided to help out voluntarily at the Mission anyway and when the job came up again, she was ready.

Janice stayed in the position from 2008 until after I had left, resigning sometime in 2013. She believed that there were some things only the Mission could do to help people. In reflecting on her time at the Mission, Janice said:

> "…the thing was we had a plan about what we wanted to see accomplished. We worked as a team, helped each other out, even if it wasn't in our job description. We were there to help the people; if anything is going to be successful, we didn't need 'prima donnas,' we needed people that would work together. It wasn't about us, it was about them, and others around who could help. People helped people. Not only did the team help the people, but the people helped each other, friends and people they knew. We all became like a family.
>
> Often families were involved, parents became volunteers and their children became involved. People who worked at the Mission brought their families to help and the families were all known to the client families. Especially the foodbank drive, staff, their families board members and clients all worked together. We all had different ways of connecting. Each role fitted the others, there was no place where one job description stopped, and another started. This was something I experienced through TCB, the Missioner saw in me skills in working with this area. It was a stretch for a start, but I really enjoyed it."

When I asked Janice about some of the difficulties she faced at the Mission, she expressed it this way:

> "Some of the most difficult times were dealing with the people for whom the Mission was their last step. Dealing with them and not coming across as a superior person. That was difficult, but I found it OK. If a tattooed Maori man came in and wanted to give me a hug it was OK and if they need telling off when they were disruptive, I did that too. Several times I had to be quite forceful, but they often come back and apologised. Stress can make things difficult at times. I would call the police if needed and sometimes it was needed, that is what I had to do for the safety of others."

Janice and I worked well together, we were able to rely on each other, share tears at times and laughed together. I very much appreciated her role in the Mission. She was right in the beginning, it was the job for her and she was the right person. And God knew that.

There were times when I needed to be away from the Mission on leave, for family emergencies, or to attend training events and conferences.

I felt confident knowing there was such a great team of staff and very able volunteers running the Mission.

Speaking about the work we all did at the Mission was continual. I spoke at service clubs, churches and church groups, schools, and clubs, and I was present at various displays, at expos, and church services.

It was also my responsibility to report to the four church courts. Anglican Social Services and at times the Bishop (domiciled in Wellington), the Catholic Social Services through the Bishop in Palmerston North, the Moderator for the Presbyterian Church and the District Superintendent of the Lower North Island Synod for the Methodist Church.

Students

In thinking of the ecumenical nature of the Mission, we welcomed several people to train with us.

The first of these was Philip who came from the Church of Christ. This was a collaborative relationship offered to help broaden the churches involved in the Mission from just the four member churches. Phillip was training as a Christian counsellor and felt working at the Mission would help widen his experience.

Although I didn't realise it at the time, Phillip would be the first of many people who would either work as volunteers or do their practicum at the Mission or actually do part of their training with us.

Philip was followed by Sue, who was in her second year of social work training and then Bonita in her first year of social work training.

Sue went on to work in Wanganui and continued to be a very valuable advocate for older people.

Several trainee social workers joined us from an international college and one young woman, Nicola, came from Massey and reflected on her time with us.

Nicola's Story

I knew Nicola's grandfather and before he died, he shared with me that his greatest regret was that he wouldn't be able to support her through her social work training and career.

I spoke to her at the funeral and told her I was there if she needed support, and she got back in contact when she was at Massey University. After finishing her first year of the Social Work Diploma, she joined us at the Mission on each of her holidays during 2011. She wanted to be outside Palmerston North and wanted something separate from her class mates who had snapped up the local places.

Coming from a church family, Nicola liked the idea of something different, a Christian-based social service that was following the mission of Jesus in a city and she wanted to find out what that looked like. I had planned tasks so that she got the most out of the time she spent with us.

Nicola started working in the foodbank helping make up food parcels and then moved to observing interviews.

She reflected on her experience:

> "The foodbank manager showed me around and I learned some interesting skills like quickly getting to know someone through non-judgemental conversation, discerning those using or abusing the service and not just taking people on their word and the use of circular questions to clarify information given. The questioning needed to be user-friendly, not an inquisition. I realised that I could not just take people at their word.
>
> I spent a little time in the shop, when we were moving, to the new shop. ...I found it quite sad when by Christmas 2011 that shop was closed by the board and the staff made redundant.
>
> At Project Jericho where I stayed a couple of nights, and I learned to roll smokes for Peter. I took a young man to get groceries who

was on TCB and was an observer to an inspection and eviction of a resident because of drug issues."

In talking about the staff Nicola said

"I really like the staff stories, how they had benefitted from help at the Mission themselves, it was a really eclectic mix of people in Wanganui who felt that people needed support, the food was there, the housing was there, the furniture was there etc and there was this real community support, all encompassing, rather than sending them around several agencies. It had a sort of a one stop shop feel about it. This felt more friendly. Clients were dealt with mostly by one person; if others were involved they talked to each other and all worked together for the client."

Nicola shared about a night she was at Project Jericho covering for a staff member whose daughter was ill, where she learned about her crisis management skills,

"Someone was very angry because they couldn't get into their unit. Someone else was coming back who had just been evicted. Shirley-Joy had been called and I was 'it' until she arrived.

I was trying to think as there were four or five things going on at one time. As a 19 year old it was challenging to step up and figure out what to do. It was one of my first crisis situations with older people. That experience made it easier for me to reflect on my own abilities and skills and how I really calmly responded. I systematically organised everything, it was only about an hour, but an interesting hour! I reflected on this as one of my pieces of work at University."

Nicola hadn't been very well but was comfortable knowing she had coped. When I asked Nicola to describe her experience at the Mission she said:

"I really liked the community feel of it, everybody was involved with the holistic gospel of 'go and serve the poor' that Jesus put out there. It didn't mean just going and telling them the good news, it meant being involved in the social, physical and spiritual dimensions of their lives. A lot of agencies I have seen in other cities are missing … this as their services only work with one part of it, the bit their funding allows for. The Mission met the need even if it didn't have the funding for that bit."

Nicola expressed real gratitude for the opportunity she had and our willingness to take her on. She felt quite at home around the Mission. She saw that staff accepted other people's faith and beliefs, and were not judgemental.

Her experience at the Mission was her first major experience of doing something independently. She found that she could handle crises, and this helped her in her later employment.

Nicola appreciated her time at the Mission. It showed her that she could work in the community and that is exactly what she was doing at the time I interviewed her. She was a community social worker, after a stint in CYF, so she also knew how the statutory and government side of things worked.

Nicola reflects:

> "My six months (at the Mission) showed me that I very much wanted to work where I could be adaptable to the needs of the people. Rather than going with what you had funding for or what the policy dictated that you had to do. Following the needs of the people and meet those regardless of whether you get fined for it."

She had observed first-hand the struggle to keep services open,

> "It seemed that the board didn't really understand the needs of the people, they seemed to be just looking from a business perspective. Which reminds me of the contractual environment there is at the moment from government. Everything needed to be running things as a business. The new hub for Ministry of Social Development (MSD) in Whanganui is like a fortress in terms of security. It is hard to get service. The Mission always had an open door even if the things were negative, they could still come and be heard. Even though there were professionals working at the Mission, people who had used the service could come back and help and be a part of the community too and help others."

I asked Nicola what messages she would want others to have about her time at the Mission. Her response was that she experienced the Mission as grounded within the community, and adaptable to the needs of the people. She appreciated that most of the paid staff and some of the volunteers were in their late 30s to early 40s, some younger than those getting help. She experienced an overarching restorative practice that suggested that if anyone needed support, it was available and in turn could be passed on to someone else. It has been good to keep in touch with Nicola through her journey.

Although we helped in the training of several social workers, only once were we able to afford to employ a social worker and he didn't stay long as he could get better pay working for the government.

Any social worker at the Mission needed to be able to 'multi-task,' i.e. interview, put together food parcels, sell Ezee meals and be available to do many other housekeeping type jobs. We all mucked in when things needed to be done and any social worker needed to do the same.

In 2010 we had another placement for practicum through Trinity Theological College. Ian Boddy was training for Presbyterial Ministry. He spent some months in and around the Mission and the city.

This seemed the height of synchronicity to me, and a most auspicious occurrence as the paper Rev Ian Boddy presented had many unexpected benefits. Its title was "The organisation and delivery of 'Christian Social Services' through the Mission in Wanganui – a case study." More from Ian's paper in a later chapter.

Hosting visitors

From time to time we had visits from churches, local and regional service clubs, and we all found that even if it was extra work hosting people visiting the Mission it was also a pleasure. We all liked to show visitors around and let them see how important the Mission was to this community.

We were regularly visited by school groups, whose main interest was in the foodbank, they had run competitions around getting more food in for us. Some schools tried to outdo each other, we didn't mind as it was all to the benefit of the foodbank.

In 2007, we hosted the Year 10 students from the Collegiate College during their "On the loose in Wanganui" Program.

This experience led to some conversations with Te Rito Peyroux and me about enabling Methodist youth to experience life at the Mission.

SeRVNT Hood as it was called, was a pilot training event between CSSW and Tauiwi Youth of the Methodist Church of New Zealand.

The purpose of the event was for up to 16 young people (16 years of age and upward) to:

- experience how people live when they lack some of the physiological needs for survival

- develop an understanding of Diaconal Ministry/servant ministry in an ecumenical setting

- be able to reflect on that experience from a theological perspective with others, both within and outside the church, and

- to share in a church service focussed on Servant Ministry.

The learning outcomes expected by the completion of the week were:

- a better understanding and ability to share about the practice of Servant Ministry by reflecting and writing a journal about their experience

- being able to offer appropriate spiritual support to those they have met

- to identify and work with different socio and cultural groups

- to identify potential unsafe situations and have strategies to address these, and

- to lead a service of worship focussing on Servant Ministry and share their experiences during the week.

It was hoped that having done this in a church in Wanganui, they might do this in their home areas and churches. The first intake in July 2009 was a great success.

With the valued leadership of Te Rito Peyroux (who at the time was the National Tauiwi Youth Facilitator for the Methodist Church) the mission team and me. We provided a challenging week for these young people.

After reviewing the outcomes of the first course we went on to hold four more events for young people. All the participants were given hoodies with the SeRVNT Hood emblem on them.

I think we were the only ones allowed to wear our hoodies in town, as at the time there was a huge media frenzy about 'gang regalia' being worn in Whanganui and people feeling threatened.

I am reminded a time when one of the young people came down stairs in the Project Jericho unit where they lived during the week, opened the cupboard in the kitchen for breakfast and seeing only Weet-Bix and a little sugar in a plastic bag, milk in the fridge, coffee and tea, she burst into tears, as she had never seen so little in a cupboard before.

These young people were taken out of their own comfort zone for a week. They lived at Project Jericho. Ate from foodbank parcels and went to friendship meals or had Ezee meals. They helped in the foodbank receiving and shelving food. They worked at the Mission Possible Shop, going out in the van to do pick-ups of furniture and household goods.

In the evenings they had bible studies and speakers from those residents and other agency workers who wanted to share their stories.

Throughout the SeRVNT Hood Training Week the participants were encouraged to keep a journal and reflect theologically on their experiences, bringing it all together and sharing with a church congregation on the last Sunday of their experience. They expressed being challenged by the work and dedication of our team at the Mission, and sometimes brought to tears by the situations they faced.

Their experience of living at Project Jericho would go on in their minds for a long time. We were to hold six SeRVNT Hood programs and around 50 young people from all around New Zealand attended them.

There were times when businesses in town closed and their staff came out and helped at the Mission, as a sort of team building exercise, and an opportunity to give back to the community.

BNZ staff at Mission Possible Shop

"Thank you, Food Lady"

I remember the small boy at one house, who quietly met me at the gate, when I was delivering a parcel of food to his family for Christmas, along with tickets to the Christmas lunch put on each year in the Memorial Hall.

This little guy, was dressed in a singlet he had almost outgrown, grubby shorts and no shoes, leaving it clear that shoes did not often protect his feet from the outside grime. He walked in beside me to his Mum, sitting on the well-worn couch feeding his sister. When we were inside he looked up at me and said, "Thank you food lady." While his Mum apologised about feeding the baby, I let her know that was fine; me and this little guy, who had already pulled up a wobbly chair in front of the mostly empty cupboard began to take the food from the box.

Inside the cupboard there was a little powdered milk, small bags of rice bubbles and sugar, two tins of spaghetti and a tin of baked beans. He told me he liked spaghetti best.

Being the man of the house, he then escorted me out and wished me a Merry Christmas. I have never forgotten that little man and wonder what that kind of poverty did to him. Where he is now? Is he still that wonderful child/young man or if poverty changed him into an angry young man?

My encounter with him became the theme for my last Column. It was titled: *"Is your life dull and routine? Do you have more hope than the world thinks is reasonable?"*

> The Christmas season is supposed to be a time of hope, joy and fun, of eating way too much. Yet every year we're confronted by songs that aren't in keeping with the Christmas spirit. It's no myth that our stress levels certainly can go up, and the last thing a stressed, depressed Christmas reveller needs are morose songs. Try these lyrics for example: "Christmas in Prison"– This man tries to remain positive and even manages to be grateful for the fact that they're serving turkey in the prison cafeteria. However, as the song continues, you start to realise that this prisoner is heartbroken and missing the love of his life who is somewhere on the outside. No time like the holidays to remember all the lost love ones you cannot be with. "The Little Boy That Santa Claus Forgot"– this isn't going to be one of those jolly sleigh-bells-a-jinglin' Christmas tunes, but

it's possibly even worse than you'd think. Not only does the little boy not have a dad, but he has to sadly watch the other boys play with their new toys, then go home and play with last year's toys... which are broken! "Have Yourself a Merry Little Christmas"– it's no accident that every single movie featuring a character who is sad around Christmas time holidays features some version of this song playing while he quietly sits alone drinking, with a single tear rolling down his cheek. So am I ready for it, for another Christmas, or another New Year.

Maybe we can actually make a dent in poverty both here in Wanganui, New Zealand and why not around the world. Maybe we can get health care working the way it should be and people don't have to wait weeks and months in pain to get surgery. We can even work on climate change and building bridges rather than walls between our faith communities. And liberate some captives and proclaim good news to the poor. Yes! I can! Arohanui."

Wanganui Midweek, 16 December 2009.

I celebrated the years end after Christmas when for a few short days I was able to be with family. My family had gathered around me and supported the work I had chosen to do here in Whanganui and we shared the fun and frustrations of serving the city. It was never just the blood family it was those chosen ones, those amazing people who had shared my life and me theirs.

Chapter 14 — A family affair or favouritism

In my time at the Mission I often heard the word nepotism used in relation to the volunteers and staff at the Mission. It wasn't used in a positive sense.

Where did nepotism come from? A Google search showed, "the origin of the term comes from the Italian word *nepotismo*, which is based on the Latin word *nepos* meaning nephew. It also suggests the term originated with the assignment of nephews to important positions by Catholic popes and bishops."

The Cambridge dictionary defines nepotism as, "favouritism to relatives or close friends by those with power the act of using your power or influence, to get good jobs or unfair advantage for members of your own family." I am wondering if working at the Mission is really a 'good job.'

I cannot speak for what was happening before I came to the Mission, although from what I do know there were lots of times when family were involved. I understood from what others have said, the Mission was always a family affair. There were families involved in the meal teams, Anne's Place, Travel Club, Foodbank Drive, most everywhere in the Mission.

I can speak about how I saw the Mission as being a family. For me there is blood family and chosen family. So there was never just people who shared my blood, but people who said they would be there and were there. People who loved me, even when I didn't deserve it, people who laughed and cried with me. Often these people were relatives or close friends. It is exactly these for whom the term nepotism is said to apply.

I want to put forward another possibility. When we completed our accountability for previous grants, reviewed services, and began upgrading, there was a huge need for complete trust and willingness to work hard for little or no reward. This progress was critical to the future work of the Mission and it was families working long hours, often unpaid, that made it possible.

In my time at the Mission, we had Sherylee in the foodbank, her Mum Maggie in the Mission Shop, her daughter Terrylee who helped in the foodbank cleaning, stacking, bagging, being a great 'go for person' and from time to time her son Caleb helped as well.

We had Jill in the office and her sister working in the Furniture Bank.

Ngareta and her daughters were involved in the foodbank, firstly with her youngest daughter Mystery, whose health often meant that her Mum brought her into work, so she could keep an eye on her. As the other girls got older they got work experience in reception.

Ngareta and her girls Summer and Denim

How much a family we were, staff, volunteers and residents of Project Jericho were represented when unexpectedly Mystery died. We were all there to farewell her, as she was our granddaughter, daughter, sister, cousin, niece and friend. She was our beautiful angel gone too soon.

If a wife worked at the Mission the husband often came along and the same if the husbands work there. If parents were involved, then often their children and their children's friends came along too.

Aunty Anne and Uncle Bill, who along with their whānau and extended whānau were never far away and were always willing to give a hand to help whenever and wherever it was needed.

Maraea, the foodbank queen, and her sister who helped Aunty Anne with Anne's Place.

Queen of the Foodbank Maraea and her sister from Anne's Place.

Mike had his wife Sue at the Furniture Bank, were a delightful couple and as a team they worked together making sure everything was presented well.

There was my son Jared, who stepped in at the Mission Possible Shop after Mike was too unwell to continue, and his wife Lisa who was a volunteer in the Reception and then managed of the Clothing Boutique after Jill left. Their two children Jade and Jesse, helping tidy up plastic bags at the food drive, and I remember Jesse eating sausages with the Collegiate Boys. I think he may still hold the record of 21 sausages in one night.

At Christmas time our whole family joined in to help at the Christmas lunch. Jared and his team loaded everything needed into the hall on the afternoon before Christmas and then loaded everything out again after the lunch was over and everyone else had gone home. Then delivering Christmas meals to those people who could not or would not make it to the meal, because there were too many people there for them to feel comfortable.

There were times when any one of the team would deliver food parcels on a weekend or help out in an emergency, no-one got paid for these times, they just did it.

At the Christmas parade and Christmas lunch, board members and their families turned up to help. In fact, more and more families were coming along to volunteer at the Christmas lunch encouraging their children and grandchildren to help. Then they would head off home for their own Christmas celebrations.

My son from another mother, Jason and his daughter Sarah worked in the shop, until he got full time work. As he looked much like Jared he was often mistaken for my other son, hence the son from another mother bit.

Jason and Sarah's Story

In his interview Jason said,

> "I learned so much about myself during the time at the Mission. I found friendship with other people, who like me needed work.
>
> Even though a lot of the time I felt withdrawn and depressed, I realised that I was not the only person struggling with mental illness. I was accepted as I was."

Without any family in New Zealand apart from his wife's family he felt very alone. Having lost his job, he felt frightened and lonely. He needed to be busy and he had lots of 'fix it' skills, and he became a valuable team Member. He was never being paid any money but worked some long hours.

Jason worked at the foodbank and the shop, and helped in the food drives and Christmas lunch. At Project Jericho he did much of the maintenance. He helped set up the workshop at the Mission Possible Shop, repaired and presented furniture for sale, checked electrical goods and built shelving, and fixed holes in the roof when needed.

His daughter Sarah joined him when she was not with her Mum and played along with my grandchildren Jade and Jesse around the core services, with Jill's daughter Bailey, Ngareta's daughter Mystery and with the children living at Project Jericho. At other times they all went to church and youth group together and appeared in the various floats for the Mission in the Christmas parades and enjoyed afternoons at the beach.

*Sarah,
one of our Angels*

Being able to work with us helped Jason to recover and eventually to find work. He now loves his special time sharing custody of his daughter. Sarah spoke of enjoying helping in the Clothing Boutique and at the Saturday Farmers Market when we were there, arriving early in the morning and setting up the stall. She shared a story about some brownie cakes that someone brought along for morning tea at the shop, something that happened quite regularly. However, this time they had a good dose of brandy in them and she scoffed the whole square and was quite sick for the rest of the day.

She talked of her race to drink the most Powerade with Lisa. She didn't win. But most of all she liked being a fairy in the Christmas parade.

*Our other angels – Bailey, Jesse, Jason
and his daughter, Mystery, Ngareta and Jade.*

When the changes began happening around the Mission, Jason did not like what he was seeing, and the way things were happening,

"There was a lot of stress and unhappiness, the way certain board members treated the staff and volunteers. It was sad as the City Mission was there to help and the internal politics created major upheaval. I was in the middle of it but had no voice.

I tried to support the others when the shop manager and the boutique manager lost their jobs but was further confused when I was approached to work in the shop that I thought was being closed. It was all unfair and disrespected the people who worked there, both paid staff and volunteers. I was uncomfortable, and it was not right. The Mission was there to help people, if they asked for help. I did and they all helped me."

Other families involved were Dave and his family, live-in caretaker at Project Jericho for a time, and Jason who was in a social worker role, who often had his daughter to stay.

Then there was Mike and Polly and their two daughters Alison and Haley. Mike was training to take over the management of Project Jericho, and Polly worked as a volunteer in the foodbank with the girls.

Alison and Haley along with my granddaughter Jade attended the last SeRVNT Hood program ably sharing the benefits of the Mission with the others who came from out of Whanganui.

Frids came to work with us, sometime later met his wife, and after a lovely wedding, he and his wife Jane both worked at Project Jericho for a time.

Evan's Story

Janice's son Evan also came to work with us. Evan had volunteered around the Mission wherever and whenever he was needed, one of the positives of nepotism.

I write this for Evan as he died in 2016. As a volunteer at the Mission he tried to have his say about what he saw was happening. This is very difficult to do when you know that a member of your family works there. But to say nothing was more than Evan could live with. He was quoted in the *Wanganui Chronicle* in December 2011 as, "calling for the board of

Christian Social Services Wanganui to be cleaned out and replaced." He had been a support person for his Mum at the meeting when the board told staff of the radical changes it was proposing and gave out redundancy letters. Evan used the words "disgusting" and "disgraceful" the way the "Smug" board members sat and delivered the redundancy letters to the staff. He was reported in the *Wanganui Chronicle* as saying that the board had no understanding of the work the Mission did, had done nothing to help them and was behaving in a heavy-handed manner. From his observations as a volunteer his view was:

> "The work of the Mission is growing, yet this board is solely intent on making money out of everything the mission does. But you can't profit from the poor."

As a volunteer he knew that the board could not take action against him, like they could with the paid staff members.

Evan continued to work for CSSW, employed as the administrator after Janice retired, in an attempt to try to encourage the board in a better direction, but to no avail. Thank you Evan for standing up for what you believed in and trying to make a difference.

The up side of nepotism for us was that we did so much together we supported each other. When some muscle was needed to quell a potential argument, Jared and Jason, the two big fellas, looked formidable. I called them my big teddy bears, but they were very protective of the women and children around them.

The down side of nepotism for us as a family was when there were difficulties and family were seen as a threat. In this circumstance it was family off first. This was to be our experience as a family, when the board made both Jared and Lisa redundant, and then dismissed me within two weeks.

I end this chapter with a quote written by Toni Morrison, an American novelist, essayist, editor, teacher, and professor emeritus at Princeton University, who won the Pulitzer Prize and the American Book Award in 1988 for *Beloved*. I felt this quote was especially true of this community in Whanganui. I believed that nepotism was alive and well, not just in families, but in various trusts, businesses and groups around the city.

Toni Morrison said,

> "Everybody gets everything handed to them. The rich inherit it. I don't mean just inheritance of money. I mean what people take for granted among the middle and upper classes, which is nepotism, the old-boy network."

I was to find the 'old-boy' network in Whanganui and on the board a challenge, it was a strong body of men and their wives that could gather together in force. Most of them had spent their lives in Wanganui, gone to school here and now worked here and raised families here. They were on the trusts, the Council and the boards, often serving on more than one of these. They had inherited their authority through the passage of time here, they were and are powerful people.

Were family favoured? It may have seemed that way, but one of the things I knew all too well, was that when something needed doing it was often the families that arrived early, worked hard and were the last to leave.

That said there was a worrying sense in all of us about what was ahead. We were all challenged by the increasing numbers of people who were coming to the Mission for help. The numbers of people needing food and accommodation. The number of vulnerable people who seemed to not be able to cope with the political changes that rained down on them.

Chapter 15 — From nostalgia into the unfamiliar

I found myself in an unfamiliar place as 2010 began. I was feeling a little overwhelmed by the increasing needs of the people who were coming to the Mission in greater numbers each week. These figures give some idea of the growth.

	2007	2008	2009
Foodbank – the total parcels given out each year were continually rising.	1,084	1,246	1,657
Those referred to TCB	68	201	188
Bed Nights once Project Jericho fully opened	33	4,464	4,392

A lot of my time was spent supporting the dedicated staff and volunteers, as we served to the best of our ability the needs of those who came to the Mission.

In the City Missioner's Column 13 January 2010 I wrote a bit about the struggles people and the Mission faced, titled *"Misguided sympathy is dangerous,"*

"Here I am in 2010 and have worked through the first weeks of this New Year. They have been the busiest weeks I have experienced. From the Christmas lunch, a wonderful group of around 110 volunteers aged from 7 years old to well into their 80s, helped feed, entertain and wish Happy Christmas to around 400 people. Followed by the days in January with around 12 food parcels each day being requested and the difficult questions we have to ask around what happened to your money? How did you spend it, and can you prove to us that it has gone on necessities? Then there were those we had to say no to, because they have not been responsible for their spending. Often, their reaction is aggressive and abusive.

It is easy to be sympathetic, however, misguided sympathy is dangerous, because it enables people to feel sorry for themselves, yet take no action. Feeling sorry for ourselves and yet taking no action means we dig the hole deeper and have less chance of getting out of it. This creates a learned helplessness guaranteeing we will feel even more hopeless.

Sometimes here at the Mission, we need to embark on tough love. For me this means having compassion for hurting people, yet never feeling sorry for them. Whenever possible, what we do here is about helping people to help themselves.

So it is 2010 and already the pressure is on people. The recession is over according to those who know about these things, yet people on benefits and low incomes without children are continuing to struggle. Advances at WINZ must be overwhelming because we see so many people who have no entitlement available.

Which forms a question in my mind, if we don't need foodbanks, how come so many people cannot cope and present themselves for help? Can we find the answer? Let's try, this year."

Dick's Story

In a conversation over a friendship meal on a Friday, I remember when the late Dick Mansfield (an ex-board member who served on the board from 2004–2011) said to me,

"How can we, who have so much, really understand the people you work with, who make choices about survival each day? Some of these choices are so different to what I would make."

He was a wise man who acknowledged his struggles with this branch of service. As a Steward at Trinity Church he was aware of the need in the community and he first joined the Mission as a "roust-a-bout" as he called himself and gradually worked his way up to "chef de mission" from 2000. His meals were always filling with five vegetables and either mince or sausages. In summer time there were cold meats and sometimes fish pie, corned silverside or chicken to break the monotony. He was the team leader at the Trinity friendship meal and King of the Kitchen.

He was the only team leader to do his first aid certificate with us, which was appreciated by the staff as we laughed our way through medical dramas and huffed and puffed the dummy through CPR.

Dick was a solid board member throughout the time I was at the Mission. He spoke of the board as a group of people keen to keep the Mission going and was impressed with the staff. In his words, at times they were, "battering their heads against a brick wall for enjoyment," and of himself he said, "being part of the Mission broadened my outlook." Dick often popped into my office, to chat and catch up with me around how things were going at the Mission and he always asked me how I was managing too.

He was a man who did much for others and it was through him that we accessed some funding from a regular benefactor, who always stayed anonymous and worked through Dick. It was Dick's commitment as a member of the Emergency Housing Committee that helped set it up and he visited many houses when we were looking for the right space to home Project Jericho. I was lucky enough to interview him not long before he died. He said he hated watching the Mission implode, disliked the lack of trust and the polarisation. The way the board and staff were at loggerheads, it sort of broke his heart. I very much miss our chats, Dick. Thank you for your support.

I thought about what Dick had said about the decisions that our clients made, their choices around survival each day being different from what he might have decided. I understood that this might be a part of the difficulty for some board members and others in the community. When I spoke to groups of people in the community, including the schools, I noticed the gap in our community between those who have quite a lot and those who have little. It was very visible.

One of these discussions was around 'scratchies' and Lotto. How could people with little or no money buy these tickets instead of food? I understood that those with little still have hope and a winning ticket might make them rich. If they didn't get a ticket, they would always be the same. I think I understood their logic and their struggle.

A dialogue was taking place within the churches about "Breaking the Cycle," moving from a theology of 'social services' to one of 'social responsibility.'

Traditionally the social service model has seen the haves "helping" the have-nots (charity to clients); the haves sharing what they decide they can spare with the 'deserving poor;' the haves deciding who is 'deserving' and 'undeserving.' This would mean supporting people within our present social and economic context – rather than addressing the structural injustices that create the need in the first place.

A theology of 'social responsibility' – is an ethical theory in which individuals are accountable for fulfilling their civic duty. The actions of an individual must benefit the whole of society.

In this way, there must be a balance between economic growth and societal welfare and the environment.

Social responsibility as defined in Investopedia is the idea that businesses should balance profit-making activities with activities that benefit society. It involves developing businesses with a positive relationship to the society in which they operate.

I had heard a bit about this from Methodist Social Services when I reported to Synod and at a national church level. When the Breaking the Cycle, information came out I wondered how it would work in a small ecumenical Mission like ours, where we saw being able to help one person as being important. We tried to inform and educate people about the advantages of change, but for so many their sense of hopelessness was overwhelming.

I expressed this in the 17 February 2010 column in the *Wanganui Midweek* titled, *"To save one life, is to save the world in time."*

> I wrote, "I don't have to watch much television or read many papers to see how much loss of life there is in this country. Lives that are taken in the madness of jealousy, bitterness and revenge. Lives snuffed out as if they were a flame of a candle. Young lives, beautiful lives and the well-worn and wise lives of older people. I wonder, as I guess you must wonder, what is going on in our community, our country and our world.
>
> Like the words from Joy Cowley's Poem, *The Heart of Stone*, 'There are times when I've cried out, God give me back my heart of stone and a ladder, so I can climb up to my head and live there with doors and windows shut on feeling.' But what will I gain by doing this, do I become immune to the death and destruction that walks our

streets or do I do what I can to make a difference? What if we all walk in the footsteps of others and try not to be noticed behind them regardless of what they do? 'How cold and dead we would feel inside and how divided the world would remain when viewed without love in our hearts.' What if we have the courage to stand out and be counted? Again, I turn to the words of Joy Cowley, 'we have to have a soft heart, one that is always vulnerable to the love and wounding which is life, which is growth...'"

I went on leave in late February/March, a much needed break. I hadn't been able to take much leave over the last few years with the busyness of the Mission and the lack of adequate numbers of trained staff. Now we had a full complement of trained staff and enough money in the accounts to get through until the next funding round and beyond.

I had questions in my mind about how to work with the new chairperson. Something was bothering me, but it could not be answered right now and time to think was always scarce around the Mission. This holiday would be good.

I attended a Diakonia World Federation Conference in Finland (of which I was the Asia Pacific Vice President), saw family in Canada and came home refreshed.

Sadly for us, while we were away, my husband's father had died. We could not get back for the funeral, so as soon as we got back from overseas I applied for bereavement leave, so we could to go up north to be with family.

I arrived back and after an Easter Service I attended, while milling around having a cup of coffee, I was confronted by the chairperson. I was told the Mission was closing because of financial problems and I was not to go back to work, and not to contact the staff, until I had met with him later.

I was grateful that I had people around me, some who heard what he had said, or I would not have believed the chairperson would speak like this publicly but wait for a better time.

The picture was to slowly unfold when I met with the chairperson again. I was informed I was no longer the 'manager' of the Mission, and a restructure had been done in my absence, by the board. Four board meetings had taken place focussed on a strategic plan. The chairperson said this had been instigated by the Wanganui District Council.

A strategic planning team was appointed and was made up of three Presbyterian members of the board and one Anglican board member.

A new vision and mission statement had been agreed at the March board meeting (25 March 2010), and the board already had begun working towards it.

I was lucky to have a very good supervisor at the time and she was present at this initial meeting. I had always had external supervision and an agreement between my employer, supervisor and myself that should I not be coping in this front line work, we would all sit down and discuss it. Either party could instigate this meeting. I was grateful to my supervisor for being willing to be present at this meeting with the Chairperson. I had a witness to the behaviour of the chairperson as he informed me of the changes. It was not presented as a plan, so much as a decree.

The new vision statement was:

> *Empowering People Encountering Life* and the mission statement:
> "Christian Social Services Whanganui (CSSW) exists to provide,
> through advocacy and strategic alliances, an exemplary holistic
> service for people in need, which enables and empowers people
> through self-management, to embrace a greater fulfilment in life."

It didn't seem a very clear mission statement, and it seemed to have been done without any consultation with staff, clients or the agencies we had worked with over the past years. It was also confusing as I knew from the agencies I worked alongside. There were more than enough social work services in Wanganui who relied on the Mission to provide the basics. Social work agencies and counsellors could help with next steps. It all fitted around my earlier question, "What did this community need the Mission to do, that others were not doing"?

I was informed that I was not the CEO, but a City Missioner and that finance and staff management were "areas of weakness within me."

I was told the funders were driving this change, although it was never clearly explained which funders the chairperson referred to.

I was told that the current board was standing up and taking the lead. They also acknowledged that under my leadership the initial purpose and mission of CSSW had been realised and achieved.

How they came to this understanding was also not explained to me. I understood everything had been working well, until the new chairperson came in along with new board members.

I was concerned for the staff and when given a chance to speak, I asked, "Who will tell the staff what is going on?" I was told that the board was looking for someone to come and help them with the process from this point on. That never happened.

There appeared to have been little or no consultation with all the churches, and only some of the board members.

I was given a copy of the minutes and documents accumulated while I was away. The chairperson informed me that he would now be the public face of the mission. He would be attending the Safer Community Meetings and any Council meetings.

Interestingly I remembered a comment the chairperson made the year before, when he asked my view on him standing for the District Council. My answer had been that as a new person to this community, maybe it would be good to get to know this area a little first. Wanganui was a city that often behaved like a small town and was often quite incestuous, it takes time to be accepted here.

The meeting with the chairperson was very unpleasant, and I was left with deep concerns for the future of the Mission and more questions than answers.

I was later told that the board was employing a manager/CEO. I was presented with an outcome from the board that would see the Mission become an exemplary social work agency, with three social workers and a Social Work Supervisor. There was no place for a City Missioner and no consultation about what happens next.

I had been told by the chairperson that I was responsible for the financial situation that the board faced. Even though it was the responsibility of the board was to raise the funds, they had never done this.

I remember Betty Bourke at several AGM's informing the board that it was one of their responsibilities to raise the needed funds to support the work of the Mission.

At the first fundraising committee meeting since I had started in 2004, held in January 2010, it seemed clear to me the selected board members had no idea how fundraising was done, what the processes and procedures were for applications, nor an understanding of the funding calendar.

This was fast entering the arena of constructive dismissal. After discussing this with some past CSSW board members and legal advisers, I decided that a personal grievance on the basis of constructive dismissal was the only option the board had left me.

Back at the Mission it seemed to be business as usual and with the annual general meeting (AGM) looming up on 14 May my report needed to be finalised. The chairperson informed me that I had to pass all information in my report to him prior to the meeting, something I had never had to do before. There seemed little time to reconnect with the staff, but they were a great bunch, knew their jobs well, and had managed everything in my absence.

We continued to face an increase in the numbers of people seeking our service. Already we were up nearly 500 first-time people seeking our help, above the total for the whole of 2009.

This year was different. Since the change in chairperson in 2009, the relationship between governance and management was becoming more and more strained. When trying to work with the chairperson at regular meetings, as I had for the past few years, things were different. I felt the pressure to do things that deep inside me I believed were not the correct. Decisions, especially around changing the core services, staffing and volunteers, were discussed that I believed risked people's safety.

Maybe, as the chairperson said, I had got too close to the staff and needed to be more like a CEO/Manager, more cut throat, like he had been when he insisted on being in a meeting with myself and a staff member over a disciplinary issue.

My decision had been to look at training for this staff member, and to find them work less isolated while this training was done. The chairperson looked the staff member in the face and asked if the staff member wanted to be at the Mission. The staff member's answer was, "Not while things are like this," to which the chairperson told him to leave.

I waited with baited breath for some weeks expecting a personal grievance from that staff member. I felt bad that it had been handled that way.

I always found people worked better when consulted with and given clear feedback. I believed I always looked for win/win outcomes, rather than dictating the outcome I might have wanted. There were times when I had to make tough decisions, and times when people didn't agree with my decisions. In the end the outcomes of some of these decisions rested heavily on me.

I had come to enjoy the reduction in the average age of the staff and volunteers from 60 to 45 years in the five years I had been the City Missioner. I always appreciated their questioning and willingness to accept change, if it came with a clear rationale. A dictatorial and bullying manner would have been met with resistance and little progress would have been made.

The synergy that had permeated the previous years was now at risk.

The sense of doing all we could, as best we could, for as long as we could, was darkened by this dark cloud of change that hovered over us. I did my best to support the staff and volunteers.

I have attended many AGMs in my 30+ years of working with non-government agencies. I was seldom just an observer and was often in a management or governance role.

The previous AGMs of CSSW had been an opportunity to report on the work of the Mission, report on the finances, celebrate the work of the Mission, field questions from the public, and introduce any new members of the board.

This AGM was to be the worst I had been at since becoming City Missioner. With the format changed and the different style of chairperson, I struggled to feel like I was even part of the process.

I would give my report as usual but was told I could not speak at any other time. That the board's new strategic direction would be presented as the highlight, not the work of the Mission. Behind much of what the chairperson said, was the "dire financial situation," and the constant reminder that without more money, the Mission could not continue.

We had never had exactly the amount needed to run the Mission at the beginning of the financial year. Yet we always made it through and were considerably better off than some of the non-government organisations in Wanganui.

In our accountability to funders we were always challenged about our investments. On the years when we ran at a small loss, we drew on these and so had never gone into debt. We lived by faith. Let me explain.

My Faith

Faith is a state of mind for me where we trust or believe something that is not necessarily possible to be certain about. It is the belief in those things which we do not see. We believe in the existence of objects which are invisible, and we are influenced by them. To walk by faith is to live in the confident expectation of things that are to come; in the belief of the existence of unseen realities.

I see that people of this world are mostly influenced by the things that are seen. They live for money, possessions, kudos, beauty, and praise, objects which this world can furnish. They behave as if there were nothing which is unseen, or as if they ought not to be influenced by the things which are unseen.

To me, faith is close to hope, but it is more concrete: we can hope to win the lottery, but it's considered a bit extreme to have faith that we will win. They do work hand in hand, as our hopes can lead to faith, and our faith can lead to new hopes.

I have found that some Christians live their lives giving lip service to faith. They never learn to trust the goodness of God and they seldom learn to hear the voice of God. So, it is when the guard rails fall off and a comfortable existence is removed, that the goodness of God can be made manifest. Sometimes in the crises of life, we lurch about, crying in desperation, "God, where are you?" only to be startled into a state of spiritual wakefulness when we get an answer, "I am here."

There are many things in the world that might suggest that God is not real or doesn't care, but that is where faith takes over for the lack of proof or the conflict of proof.

Having faith in God means that we trust that the Creator is there and that there is a greater scheme in mind than what we can actually see or understand, in spite of evidence to the contrary.

The interesting thing about all this for me was that the predominantly non-church-going staff had a deep faith and strong hope in the understanding that if we did the right things well, then we believed that the money would be available. This had worked over the past six years for us and we believed this would continue and it did. Miracles did happen.

The day of the AGM loomed up, I found myself spending time sitting alone and asking God for an answer to this struggle. With the meeting to start at 7.30pm, I was collecting dinner from the Noodle Canteen, when my phone rang. A person whom I had never met, and never did meet in person, who lived in the South Island, asked me this question, "Is the financial situation the only reason that the Mission is struggling." Wanting to 'toe the party line' I said, "Yes." This man then offered to deposit a substantial sum of money into the Mission Account the next business day. For me it was an answer to prayer; a sign, hope that if we continued to do the right things then the money would be there for it.

I asked if this man would send an e-mail to me at work, to confirm this gift, and if I could share this with the meeting tonight. He agreed. This was done.

So, amidst the struggle, animosity and distrust at the AGM came an answer to prayer. This was recorded in the Minutes of the AGM under City Missioner's Report:

> "Shirley-Joy City Missioner said it was good to celebrate the work of the Mission. She shared the news of a miracle that had occurred this week. Donation of $50,000 to support the Mission and another $30,000 for food production had been received."

It was some months later, that the administrator told me that the chairperson presented a cheque for $50,000 from another anonymous benefactor dated before the AGM. Did this mean we now had

$100,000 and the funding round just starting for the year, and yet the board was still talking of the "dire financial situation?"

It seemed that financial provision had been received for the Mission to get through the year, and maybe beyond, without a deficit.

The AGM and the events leading up to it had taken their toll on me. After the meeting I did something I had often done in the past, I ran and hid from the world.

My emotions bubbled over and as I sat in the darkness of a building in town, much like I used to do when I lived on the street. I cried and sobbed until the emotions had drained from me. Exhausted I walked home through the misty streets of this city I had begun to love.

In the light of a new morning, as the sun rose, the Mission had to go on. So many people needed the services we provided. It was not just me and how I was feeling. Most of those who worked at the coal-face of the Mission were feeling unsettled and concerned about the unfamiliar ground we were now forced along. The staff were open to change if things are not working, and often in the past we had looked at doing things differently when needed.

Next morning speaking to the staff we all agreed that it was a 'we' situation; board, management, staff, volunteers and our community, make up the 'we' that is the Mission.

However, as the newspapers often do, the *Wanganui Chronicle* carried this story the next day. The headline was: *"Christians split in row over Mission written by Kathryn King."*

> "Simmering tensions over the future of the City Mission have led to a serious rift among Christian factors in Wanganui.
>
> The row has been triggered by proposals from the CSSW board to radically change the City Mission's staffing structure.
>
> In his report, board chairman the Reverend Gene Lawrence told the meeting the City Mission could not afford another financial loss as high as last year's $63,000 deficit. He said rationalisation and restructuring were required.
>
> A new mission statement, to move the mission's services in a "primarily social work and relationship based" direction was

unveiled, as was an accompanying staffing structure to help implement the changes.

Under the new structure two new key positions would be created – a "mission manager" reporting to the board chairperson, and a "social work supervisor" who would oversee it what was hoped would be an increasing team of social workers (sic).

"The distinct difference is that we no longer exist to provide and/or create services to meet the needs of people in our community. Rather we seek to address the reason the need exists in the first place," Mr Lawrence said.

Where City Missioner Shirley-Joy Barrow would fit into the structure was not made clear.

Current services provided by the mission, which "might" fit into the new direction of the mission were the foodbank, Project Jericho (emergency and temporary housing) and the furniture bank.

The other services of the mission, which include budget management, meal deliveries, friendship meals, a drop-in centre and low-cost travel club, were under review.

It was made clear that the restructuring could mean redundancies of paid staff and volunteers.

The announcement was met with criticism from a number of people at the meeting, who questioned the board's methods in creating and introducing the proposed staff structure.

When faced with the criticism, Mr Lawrence asked at least two members of the public to leave.

While staff have now been asked to make submissions on the proposed changes, foodbank coordinator Jeanette Prior said they had not been consulted in the creation of the proposed restructuring.

Emergency housing volunteer and former board member John Penny said he felt Mr Lawrence's actions were "dictatorial" and called the board "out of touch with reality."

[Board financial officer Tim] Campbell admitted that a financial analysis had not been completed and it would likely cost more money than the current arrangements. "If it's not economically viable, then why sell the idea?" [Methodist minister Rev Tony] Bell asked.

Mr Bell said the best thing the board could do was to start again, making sure all the partner churches and staff were consulted.

"A bit of Christian grace is needed here, bearing in mind the people we are trying to help. I think it's a sad day when they hear something they don't like they try to have them removed. Where's the open accountability?"

Wanganui Chronicle, 16 May 2010.

Neither the chairperson, nor I, would find the months ahead easy, as trust had been lost. The work at the Mission and the work of the board seemed to be going in two completely different directions.

Chapter 16 — Polarisation

Covenant of trust

"A covenant is a type of contract in which two people or organisations make a promise to do or not do some action. We make contracts in our everyday life. Every time we hand over money, stop on a red light, or go on the green light – we do so assuming that this covenant will be kept by others as well. Ever found yourself sitting on a red light in the early hours of the morning with no-one else around. Why not go – because we live by mutual covenants. Society is made workable by voluntary compliance which is often unenforceable. When we drop our children off at school we are part of a covenant of trust with the school and teachers. When we are in a relationship with each other, even when the terms of the relationship maybe unspoken. This is so real at the City Mission, we are constantly in relationship with so many people who ask our help in their struggle to survive. They sign an agreement with us to help them and they agree to find ways to live as best they can, with what they have.

So if we want peace, and if we still believe in justice, then we must change more than our administration. We must recover conscience and reject the dominant desires for personal victory. And this cannot happen without a renewed sense of covenant – covenants which are made on trust and not fear. Arohanui."

City Missioner's Column, Wanganui Midweek, 2 June 2010.

With the annual general meeting over and continued difficulties, I struggled with the thought of what was ahead of me. When I went into work, little had changed, the usual things to be done, the unexpected to be taken in my stride, and all the time I felt like I was watching out for a sideswipe.

The staff gathered around, and we processed the fall-out from the meeting with the board. The friendship meal team leaders were unsettled with the accusations about their handling of the money they used for buying supplies and the donations they received. We were all a little bit shell-shocked.

However, we were resilient and had faith that if we continued to do the right thing, provision would be received for the needs our clients faced.

In the busyness of the Mission I had missed the growing power of the politics of the day, and the tentacles that were reaching into the Mission. As the two main parties prepared for an election next year, the Mission continued to fight the injustices that had crept in and the growing poverty amongst those on low and fixed incomes.

It was at this time that Rev Ian Boddy was doing his practicum from Trinity Theological College and he has given me permission to use parts of his paper, *The organisation and delivery of "Christian Social Services" through the Mission in Wanganui – a case study.* (Mentioned in Chapter 13.) I believed that Ian grasped the difficulty we faced during this time at the Mission and expressed it well.

In his introduction to the paper, Ian wrote:

> "In July (2010) my planned placement went ahead, and things carried on 'as normal' at the community interface level, while in the background there was turmoil at the governance and management levels. By October when my placement ended the everyday practices continued as they had all year. Changes were still in the air, but with much reduced tension following the resignation of the board chairperson."

Ian was so right, when the then chairperson resigned, I felt like a huge weight had lifted from me. I could at last focus on the work of the Mission again, as I had done all the way through these challenging years of being City Missioner. Rev Boddy was also right when his paper focussed on the other ongoing struggle, that of structural injustices.

Ian wrote, "I was aware of the Welfare Working Group that was established in April 2010 and the National Government's desire to break the cycle of dependency." He knew as we knew that a "drastic reduction of dependency" would put huge demands on the Mission.

As Ian detailed in his paper:

> "It is a financial imperative coming out of neo-liberal economic theories. The government has introduced some changes from 27 September this year:

- Sole parents with no children under six may have their benefits halved unless they seek part time work.

- Sickness beneficiaries judged to be capable of part-time work will be work-tested from next May.

- A new medical certificate will be used from September 27 to move invalid beneficiaries on to sickness benefits if they will be able to work part-time in the next two years.

- A Government working group is looking at other changes to cut long-term welfare dependence.

These moves to blame the poor for their plight are miserly enough but are reinforced by institutional attitudes which make people uncomfortable in attending WINZ to ask for their rightful entitlements.

The *New Zealand Herald* reported beneficiary's responses to recent visits to WINZ:

- A lack of compassion

- Their whole attitude towards me has changed. Each time I go in there they are quite abusive

- Cold and depersonalised

- Can't ring them on a direct line any more. You have to ring the call centre.

- Broke down in tears.

- Might end up out on the street.

Similar people are City Mission's clients. Foodbank applicants need a letter from WINZ saying that they have no further food assistance entitlement. I observed in recent weeks that clients were experiencing difficulty obtaining the necessary letter from WINZ. There is indeed 'structural injustice.'"

It was only as time went by that I fully appreciated Ian's paper, and his way of summing up such a difficult time from his perspective of working and living within the work of the Mission. At the Mission we responded to the people who came to us, people with nowhere else to turn.

Since August 2010, my personal grievance had been with the Department of Labour awaiting mediation. This was resolved at mediation on 22 March 2011, which included engaging a suitable person in the role of Mission Co-Ordinator, with fundraising a high priority for this role.

I had agreed to this change of Mission structure and role description as a way forward. I was glad the board was now going to focus on its governance role of fundraising. However, this caused some further unrest as it seemed that part of the administrator's role was now at risk.

The board seemed still committed to the new plan devised by the previous chairperson and the newly created position of Mission Co-ordinator did not start immediately, nor did the board have a salary for this position.

Needless to say, I found myself with more and more to do, often involving meetings with the board where I was questioned as to why funding applied for by the mission co-ordinator was unsuccessful. Respectfully, I suggested they ask the co-ordinator. This voluntary Mission Co-ordinator attended some meetings and then went away for quite a period of time overseas, leaving the administrator and I to continue to do what we had always done regarding the funding.

The next steps taken by the board were a training day on governance, followed by a strategic planning process which suggested that, "To be successful strategic planners – Plan, Implement THEN Monitor and Review REGULARLY."

The board was busy rewriting their constitution, reviewing the core services, all of which was part of their role. They even attempted to form a fundraising committee. I spent time briefing the fundraising committee on the funding calendar and processes we had followed, which they experienced as being very complex.

I anticipated some clear direction as to what they required of me other than business as usual, meeting the growing demand from the community for the services we provided.

As the board members went and visited around the core services reviewing each one, a staff member present at one such visit commented, "that the visit of the board was like the henchmen for the Grim Reaper with scythe at the ready." Staff and volunteers felt a sense of doom over what was asked and what was said to them by board members. They were also concerned at how little the board knew of how the Mission operated and linked core services.

I was concerned about this as I had run yearly orientation opportunities after each AGM for new board members and tried to clarify any concerns and answer questions they may have had.

I sensed the presence of the previous chairperson although the new chairperson went to great lengths to assure me, "that was over, and we could trust each other and move forward together." I remembered the chairperson saying one time in the staffroom, that the Mission was, "his church now." I felt shivers then, because that didn't seem right to me. My belief was we go to church to be refreshed and energised to go out and serve. Those same shivers came again and again as time went on.

My disquiet continued, and it seemed that so much of what I did now was being challenged. In my time at the Mission I had only had one complaint and this one had been decided, in my absence, by the board, and when I returned from leave I sought redress of their decision which was done, and a letter given to me.

> "It was agreed that the Board's response lacked good due process and that the Board didn't full investigate the complaint. We acknowledge this wrongdoing. And the hurt it caused you. We are sorry and ask for your forgiveness. The current Board is beginning to work well together and are in full support of you and the work of the Mission. We would like to assure you that steps are being taken to ensure that a robust grievance/complaints process is being developed so that you and the Mission will be safeguarded in the future."

The letter was signed by the chairperson and dated 26 June 2009.

In the middle of 2011, from June through to September, I was to face four complaints. Each one seemed to be grasped eagerly by various board members. I believed they were out to find reasons to take disciplinary procedures against me. I spent more time watching my back than I did undertaking the work I was committed to. The staff began to see what was happening, although I tried to spare them from the situation that was developing. As it became clear to me that the board seemed intent on closing the Mission, I knew that this was a fight for the life of the Mission as I had known it.

The political mind-set to place a business template over social services was being strongly pushed by the board. I was never sure if it was all of the board, but certainly there were strong intentions from some to go in this direction.

As the end of the year neared I was already beginning the preparations for Christmas community lunch. Planning was well on its way and donations were coming in much like the past years. The board decided to increase the cost of tickets to the meal and wanted to see cash positive figures or it would be cancelled.

> "The Wanganui's Christmas Day Community meal could be in jeopardy. The Board of Christian Social Services Wanganui, which oversees the City Mission, has concerns about the financial viability of the Mission and has introduced what it calls a series of strict management "structures and processes." The *Chronicle* has been given a copy of a letter the Board sent to staff, signed by Board Chairman Tim Campbell. Among other things, the board has asked management to prepare a detailed budget of the Christmas Day Meal, including both income and expenditure and "unless this is cash-positive it may not progress."

> *Wanganui Chronicle 26 & 27 November 2011*

The Community Christmas lunch, in the time I had been there as City Missioner, had never run at a loss, although the whole of the amount needed to run it was not always banked before December. By Christmas Day all the costs were covered. In the last two years there had been a surplus enabling us to buy big pots instead of borrowing or hiring them, keeping costs down. Four local businesses guaranteed any shortfall that might occur from this year's lunch, but the board wanted the money in the bank before they would accept this.

The write-up continued:

> "The staff have also been told that further restructuring "may be necessary before Christmas" but no decision had been made yet." "Mr Campbell said the board saw the need to protect the City Mission's core projects and would do everything it could to ensure the success of these projects."

> *Wanganui Chronicle, 26 & 27 November 2011*

Alongside this was the board's clear intention to close the Shop before Christmas and with serious plans around closing Project Jericho.

I believed I had been doing the right thing.

In my busyness in running the Mission I had not focussed on the upcoming election and I didn't fully comprehend its impact on the Mission until a few weeks before the election, when the Prime Minister John Key was in town in the National party bus. There for all to see in the Majestic Square was one of our staff members, with his Labour placard in hand, kanohi ki te kanohi (nose to nose), with a board member in his National party colours.

As always in a community there are those who agree and those that disagree. Those who see the events in their way and those who see it differently. Someone once wrote a hymn that said, "Different is beautiful, God bless variety, just look around and see – Different is beautiful." Yet there are times we fail to appreciate the differences.

As I read the newspaper articles about what people said, I realised how divided people's thinking was about the Mission and me as City Missioner.

The board would, in 2012, celebrate 20 years of service to the community. I had designed a calendar at the board's request to be sold to help with the fundraising.

Amongst all of this was an experience that I will always carry with me. I had been asked to meet with a group of intercessors from different churches around our city, who had faithfully prayed for the city for many years.

Their message was given to me as I sat in the center of their prayer circle and felt anointed by their presence.

Their message began:

> "Not a death of ministry, a phoenix rising from the ashes.
> Refreshing water will flow from me and in time there will be
> restoring of the years the locusts have eaten. The stocks will be lifted
> from my neck and the chains that have bound me will fall away and
> miracle after miracle will heal the wounded hearts."

I found it hard at the time to see the relevance and was consumed with the encroaching sense of darkness. Thankfully I was given this message handwritten on a small piece of paper.

A second piece of paper was also placed in my hand as I was about to leave. This was a scripture reference Psalm 19:1–19:

> "The Lord rewards me because what I do is right. He blesses me because I am innocent. I have obeyed the Law of the Lord: I have not turned away from my God. I have observed all his laws; I have not disobeyed his commands. He knows I am faultless, that I have kept myself from doing wrong. And so, he rewards me because I do what is right, because he knows I am innocent. Oh Lord, you are faithful to those who are faithful to you, completely good to those who are perfect. You are pure to those who are pure, but hostile to those who are wicked. You save those who are humble, but you humble those who are proud.
>
> Oh, Lord, you give me light; you dispel my darkness. You give me strength to attack my enemies and power to overcome their defences."

It would be some six months into 2012 before I was to realise the power of this prophecy. Then these words became a thread that I would hold onto in the months and years of anxiety that were ahead.

My column, entitled, *"There has to be a line beyond which you will not go. You have to know where that line is drawn,"* helped in expressing what was happening around and within me.

> "When I think about my principles, I know that without these principles I would end up despising myself. There is a line beyond which I will not go. That line for me is injustice. When faced with injustice, I cannot do anything other than fight for justice. So, this is where I draw my line. My line can sometimes feel wide and high and made of solid steel. I cannot go beyond it no matter what. I believe as Aristotle did, that "every effect has a cause," that everything that begins to exist must have a cause. Aristotle formulated that, "everything that moves is moved by another." It is a powerful argument and for me a powerful cause to defend.
>
> So where do you draw your line? I am sure, like me, you have been asked to do things you didn't like. You have even been asked to do things that are unpleasant. But whenever I have been asked to cross my own personal line – which thankfully has only been once

or twice – then it is time to say no; no more injustice; no more bullying; no more trying to pretend I don't see when injustice when is done to others. My intuition tells me this is wrong.

Sometimes it is important to follow our own intuition. Deep down we each know when we are right and when we are wrong. Often it takes courage to listen to our intuition. If we have looked at things from all sides, from all viewpoints, have got feedback from those around us and have a deep sense of where we draw the line; and we have a habit of 'listening' to how we feel; then we will make the right decisions and claim the place where we have drawn the line. Arohanui."

Wanganui Midweek, 7 December 2011.

In my last few months at the Mission I was to face a further two complaints, more restructuring, growing staff concerns about their jobs, increasing numbers of clients, along with family changes. My Mum had come to live with us and we had shifted to a house that would accommodate her too.

Family members who also worked at the Mission, who would lose their jobs just before Christmas, would see their hard work in the shop, building it up, then shifting and setting it all up again, nullified when the board closed it. This all culminated in a meeting with the board just before Christmas of staff, volunteers and their support people. Here they were told of the closures that the board had now had decided upon.

Immediately following this meeting, a board member reported to the Police that I had physically abused a board member at the meeting. The situation seen by the 20 of us left inside the meeting went like this.

After the board had been heard and a number of the staff were quite bereft, I asked if the board had any more to say. They didn't, so I encouraged the board to leave the room, so the staff could debrief.

A board member stood up and told the staff that she had never met any people less Christian than this lot. The staff reacted to that, one person stepping up to verbally challenge her. I shepherded the board member out of the room, just as the chairperson, who had already left, returned and bumped her into me. This became the fifth complaint. No charges were laid by the Police.

A number of staff, including me, drafted letters to the board regarding what we believed was constructive dismissal.

It was over. The board seemed to have achieved what they set out to do in pursuance of their desire, "to provide, through advocacy and strategic alliances, an exemplary holistic service for people in need, which enables and empowers people through self-management, to embrace a greater fulfilment in life" and set up a social work agency.

They had begun dismantling the core services of the Mission, tearing away hopes and dreams. The board with its bureaucratic mind-set was committed to its direction, no matter what.

The stress on staff and some volunteers was unimaginable, with bereft staff struggling to do their best and waiting for the 'chop' right at Christmas.

Cartoon by Murray Crawford.

I believed the board's desire was clear, to follow the party line and make this social service into a business. To only "do the necessary" and a little of what was easily possible.

I was contacted by a *Wanganui Chronicle* reporter and asked for comment. In my frustration, having heard from the reporter that he had just spoken to some members of the board that I "would be gone by Friday," and "not to print anything I said without their (the Board's) approval." This included the regular column in the *Wanganui Midweek*, and this was "because I was dysfunctional."

I replied that if anyone was dysfunctional, it was the board. This became front page news on election day and the sixth point for disciplinary action.

I could not continue to work with this board: those who made the decisions and those who went along with the decisions. Even the past

Local poor taking brunt of economic downturn, says City Mission

By Anne-Marie Emerson

"These are people who do not have any family or friends they can turn to, especially where food, clothing and furniture are involved."

– City Missioner Shirley-Joy Barrow

The economic downturn is hitting Wanganui's poorest residents hard according to the City Mission.

City Missioner Shirley-Joy Barrow recently presented a report on the state of the City Mission to the Wanganui District Council's Community Development Committee.

Ms Barrow stated the facts: between January and March 2008, 11 families required a food parcel for the first time; between January and March 2009 that figure was 35.

Demand for emergency help such as that offered by the City Mission has tracked upwards over the past few years, Ms Barrow said.

Families with children requiring food parcels was 560 in 2006, 1206 in 2007, and 1117 in 2008.

Families requiring furniture and clothing increased from 34 to 43 between 2006 and 2008.

Ms Barrow said by the time a family reached the City Mission they were usually in a desperate situation.

"These are people who do not have any family or friends they can turn to, especially where food, clothing and furniture are involved, and have exhausted all advance entitlement available through [WINZ], or, if they are or have been employed, have used all the resources available to them.

Under the Community Contract, the council gave $6500 annually to the City Mission.

"Which in the scheme of things is not that much."

Ray Stevens, chair of the Community Development Committee, said the council was concerned for the City Mission's plight but said "we're not quite sure how we can help."

"We're hoping the mission will come back to us with suggestions of ways we can help further."

The committee recommended the council lobby central government to increase the accommodation allowance level for Wanganui.

"At the moment it's only $45 and in other towns similar to Wanganui it's $65."

Source: *Wanganui Chronicle 22 April 2009*

board members felt the need to be heard in the days that followed and the depth of the polarisation echoed in the community.

In the *Wanganui Chronicle* letters to the editor on 1 December 2011, under the heading *Mission Crisis*, Shirley W McGrath wrote:

> "As one of many who have freely given their time and effort as members of the board of Christian Social services Wanganui, I was appalled to read the front page article "City Mission in crisis" *in the Wanganui Chronicle (26 November)*.
>
> There are two sides to this story. I resigned from the board after some six years, because I could no longer tolerate the negative responses of the present City Missioner, an employee of the board, to the directives and recommendations of the board. In all sincerity, I suggest that if, as she claims, "she could walk away," then in the interests of both herself and the board that might be a charitable thing to do."

Wanganui Chronicle, 1 December 2011.

The late Harvey Hoskin, a board member who had only recently retired from the Board, wrote a letter to the editor which said:

> "I wish to express my disappointment and indeed anger at the continued perverse failure of the Christian Social Services board to recognise the responsibilities, as part of its governing governance functions, to develop the financial resources (i.e. fundraise) for the essential working of the management aspect in meeting and relating to people with real basic needs. As one who as a past member (Methodist) on that board, I recognised "governance" as not being among my abilities and resigned from that position so that it could be occupied by someone more able and inclined. This was after I discovered, and clearly and openly stated at the board meeting, that one of its tasks was to fundraise and not to leave it to management (those working at the coal face) to do all the necessary fundraising. But it was ignored and never recorded, despite the general understanding that fundraising is part of governance functions. Shirley-Joy has held the position of City Missioner for the past eight years and has unstintingly been constantly available, being called out at all hours to listen to and meet people in their need(s). An amazing amount of work is involved and even gaining financial support from various voluntary donors for the needy encountered.

There is certainly a need to replace the current board with members who are informed, willing and able, dedicated to a fair deal for all, and in contact with the reality of the needs of folk requiring the assistance of caring discerning listeners. A reference from a board member's namesake is found in 1st Timothy Chapter 6, verses 10, 17–21. How the injustices prevailing can be approved in the light of this, I cannot understand. Also, I must say that periodically I meet past members of the City Mission board (Methodist, Presbyterian and Catholic) and gather they too are concerned over the welfare of those in need, and who have felt the frustration of the board's constant inefficiency. It is no wonder Shirley-Joy is feeling abandoned and got-at.

It is not the money which is at the root of all evil – but the "love of money" – being more than the love/care of people, especially people in real need. How the board of the Whanganui Christian Mission can fall into that old trap is a constant source of amazement and disappointment. It is an age old problem, as is indicated by the above reference from Paul's letter to Timothy – about 2000 years ago.

Basically, a fair deal for all – i.e. justice administered in love/care – is what is required here. The mission board seems to have become so obsessed with its own self-delegated authority, rather than that of Jesus and the way he lived, taught and died in defence of. This is what we are called to follow."

Wanganui Chronicle, 8 December 2011.

A group of past board members entered in with a letter given to the *Wanganui Chronicle,* used in an article that appeared on 5 December 2011, written by John Maslin, entitled *"CSSW members react to criticisms."*

"A group of life members and former chairmen of Christian Social Services Wanganui (CSSW) have rallied in support of the present board which has been strongly criticised by the City Missioner. 'Missioner Shirley-Joy Barrow described the board as dysfunctional and said it did not understand what it was doing and needed to be replaced (*Chronicle,* 26 November)'.

Now, in a letter to the *Chronicle,* six people said they expressed their "deep resentment" with the *Chronicle* story. They include Heather Russell, Betty Bourke, George Bowers, Graeme Carter, Michael Coleman and Brian George.

Mrs Barrow, who has been City Missioner for the past eight years, told the *Chronicle* she was prepared to walk away from her job because of the constant battles she was having with the board.

She said the board should be replaced with an interim board to get things sorted out, "because this board has been dysfunctional for the eight years I've been here and longer," and now "it's become a real battle between them and me."

Mrs Barrow said she believed the board was trying to put a business template on the social service.

But the letter's signatories said they strongly backed the board and what it was trying to do. And this involved the City Missioner carrying out policy as directed by the board.

"The City Missioner's apparent almost complete lack of loyalty to, and respect for, the board as her employer, as expressed in the (*Chronicle*) report, we deplore."

They said the board and missioner must understand the roles of governance and management "and it seems there is neglect of this by the City Missioner, despite the best efforts of the board."

And they rejected Mrs Barrow's claim of a major disconnect between the mission and the board because churches received regular oral and written reports at their governing bodies' meetings.

"While the City Mission has a social agenda, it must be run as a business and its functions must be carried out in accordance with the finances of the board.

"The Missioner has no understanding of business practice and furthermore does not wish to be bound by such."

They said the founding churches appointed members to govern CSSW. They all continued to contribute financially and with many voluntary hours and donations of food and other items to ensure this was done in a businesslike way to meet the needs of many Whanganui people.

"A business template is a necessity for any group spending public money, not to be decried, as the Missioner stated in the report.

"Not to have such would destroy public confidence in the work of any organisation," the six said."

Wanganui Chronicle, 5 December 2011.

The Mission, emergency housing and the mission shop employed a total of 10 paid staff, while there were 100 volunteers.

The board comprises three people from each of the four main churches, Anglican, Catholic, Presbyterian and Methodist; who gave $6,000 a year to the mission.

This reminded me of what Rev David Day had commented regarding the then board's governance responsibility for fundraising and that the initial giving from the churches when the Mission was started. "Each affiliated member was required to pay an annual levy of $12,000 in 1992, a total from the churches of $36,000." This was initially for three churches and when the fourth came on board I would assume they also paid $12,000 giving a total of $48,000.

By 1992 this amount had been reduced to $8,000 per church per year. When I began at the Mission, as it had been in tenure of Rev David Day, fundraising was left to the City Missioner. In the time from 1992 to 2004 costs had substantially risen, but not the contribution from the churches and at times it was difficult to know exactly when that money would be received, some churches choosing to drip feed it over the year and some depositing their amount in a lump sum.

I acknowledge that there were volunteers from those churches that gave their time and some churches gave food collected at Sunday service all this was greatly appreciated.

In some cases, church property was available for the Mission's use without charge or with a small rental to cover insurance, power etc. We were always enthusiastic when church members visited and spent time seeing what we did and having a cuppa with us, which happened from time to time.

We also received regular phone calls telling us the things our clients were seen doing, having been recognised in the community after being seen visiting the Mission.

As an ordained minister myself, I knew the difficulties most of the churches faced with aging and declining church membership. I also understood the contracting processes that the MSD, the health service and other government agencies were using. Finding ways to tap into this funding was very much a full-time job in itself. Accountability for each dollar received also had to be done, something that was in arrears when I started.

Fundraising was accepted as a clear responsibility of the board, as evidenced in a Letter to the Editor in the *Wanganui Chronicle* 2012, from Life Member the now late Mr George Bowers, "As a Member of the Board when the Mission was established, care was taken to build up the monetary reserves to meet any emergency."

I do agree with the writers of the letter to the *Wanganui Chronicle* that:

> "While the City Mission has a social agenda, it must be run as a business and its functions must be carried out in accordance with the finances of the board."

However, if that had been followed, the Mission was not viable when I was employed, nor were there clear governance policies. As to their suggestion I had no understanding of business practice, I held strongly to the faith I had that if we did the work well, God would provide, and God did, often in rather miraculous ways.

My disappointment was that most of the people named in the article had not been in the Mission for years (some had attended AGMs) and none ever bothered to come and talk with me to see if there might have been two sides to this situation.

Then there were other views. Mr John Penny, also a past board member wrote a letter to the editor – entitled *"Destroying goodwill."*

> "Mr Reon Suddaby (*Chronicle* Editorial, 16 December), why can you clearly state the obvious fundamental flaw in the CSSW board's thinking, yet they themselves cannot? I was a board member some years ago and a volunteer in many aspects of their good work. I have not received one cent for the hundreds of hours of free work. I have just helped at a lunch for approximately 40 vulnerable people of our community who enjoyed an excellent lunch, which turned a small profit but which the board know very little about, having never spoken to those involved. Just another example of a shameful managerial practice (i.e. making decisions without full facts). The board must resign en masse, as it is destroying Christian goodwill built up over 20 years. It is time for all of them to be named and shamed. I am ashamed, through my Christian commitment, to have this board tarnish our belief in caring for others."
>
> *Wanganui Chronicle, 20 December 2011.*

I needed a distraction to stay sane and it came. A young man whom I had been close to in a previous parish was dying of cancer, and he had asked his Mum and Dad if I could take his funeral when he died.

I went away to the Waikato to sit by his bed in his last days and to farewell him from this earthly life. That for me is servant ministry.

I penned my last column as City Missioner when the board was intent on cancelling the community Christmas lunch. It was titled, *"The Whos young and old would sit down to a feast, and they'll feast, and they'll feast." Dr Seuss.*

"I am sure you recognise this quote, every Christmas someone brings out the book, written by Theodor Seuss Geisel the American writer, poet and cartoonist, who wrote under his pen name Dr Seuss. He was inspired to write.

On return voyage from Europe he used the rhythm of a ship's engine to inspire a poem and his first book. During World War II, he was known for his political cartoons, posters and for commanding the Animation Department of the First Motion Picture Unit of the United States Army Air Forces.

After the war was over he returned to writing children's books that parents and children enjoyed. Even though he never had any children himself, he is known to have said, "You have 'em; I'll entertain 'em."

For me, the Grinch stealing Christmas, is his best. The Grinch is a fictional character, a bitter, cave dwelling creature with a heart "two sizes too small", living on snowy Mount Crumpit, a steep, 910 metre mountain just north of Whoville, the home of the merry and warm hearted Whos. Hearing the joyous sounds of Christmas, an annoyed Grinch plans to take away the Whos' happiness and deprive them of Christmas. The Grinch then realises that Christmas is more than just gifts and presents, it is about family and friends. Touched by this, his heart grows three sizes larger; he returns all the presents and is warmly welcomed into the community of the Whos.

So what am I saying? As we draw ever closer to Christmas there will be the 'Grinches' and the 'Whos.' I want to encourage every Grinch out there; that people care about you, don't want you to be alone and want you to have a good Christmas too. Maybe you can leave your bitterness behind, come down from your mountain cave and be touched (growing your heart three times bigger). Come on down. Arohanui."

Wanganui Midweek, 14 December 2011

There was no more I could do for the Mission, I was relieved in some ways to be out of the pressure and stress. I actually had my first Christmas with family on our own since 2005.

Just one last thing. The gossip (and there was always lots of gossip around the Mission) and accusations of misappropriating Mission money were heard around the city, which was the reason that a newspaper notice was requested from the board. It read,

> "The board wishes to clarify that at no time during her employment was there any misappropriation of funds or theft of any property by the former City Missioner, Shirley-Joy Barrow."

I reached settlement with CSSW under Section 149 Employment Relations Act 2000, in September 2012. The following notice was published in the *Wanganui Chronicle*. With a positively worded written reference from the board, ending with, "The Board wishes Shirley-Joy well for the future," I believed that episode in my life was now over.

I never requested or accepted any financial settlement as I believed that it would be taking money from the most vulnerable in our community.

I never left this city, though some thought we had moved away. I did go through a time when my life seemed over, when I could not get employment, when the board continued its support of one of the complaints through my professional body and then through the church.

My heart was broken, I was exhausted, but I never gave up caring for those who also experience brokenness, exhaustion and loss of hope.

I continued to dream about what was ahead, what would happen to me next.

Chapter 17 — Reflect, Review and Respond

I wrote things down, thinking over what had happened, trying to process all the things that had gone on in a short period of time, and wondering what I could have done differently. This is taken from my journal on the first day of January 2012:

> "I am finding it very hard as things go by, day by day. Friends and staff ask about what is happening. Little snippets are relayed to me and I go again on that roller-coaster of strength to sadness to anger. Being dismissed because I went to the press and declared what I believed was the truth about the board's incompetence, seems unfair. Some people tell me I have done the right thing, others are condemning. I move from a deep sadness that I am no longer part of this, to anger that this ever happened. I trusted people with so much and now I feel betrayed. Was I wrong in what I did? Now I don't have a job, seem to have lost credibility, and am desperately sad."

Review and Reflect

As time went on I reviewed what I had done during my time at the City Mission.

In applying for the position as City Missioner I believed that I was the right person for the role at that time. I sensed that although I had had no wish to be in Wanganui (then without the 'h'), this position offered me a journey into management I had hoped for and in some ways dreamed of. That dream was to lead a team of committed, passionate people to serve others, to gently challenge people within the church (regardless of denomination) to see that their journey into mission started when they left the church building, after energising and preparing themselves through worship and fellowship.

I had begun with enthusiasm and excitement and listening to the heartbeat of the city. I had noticed the ebb and flow of the community, of unique people who lived and had lived beside this majestic river for hundreds of years, growing, trading, educating and working. That mix of cultures both ethnic and socio-economic, of many religions, great schools, sports and the arts.

I had entered into what I believed was a cycle of hope for people who struggled the most in this place with a larger than most beneficiary community.

I believed I had a clear picture of the direction, the founders of the Mission had some ten years earlier. I had accepted the role as City Missioner which clearly was to:

- Provide leadership to the organisation

- Develop and enhance initiatives that fall within the ethos of the organisation, and

- Raise and maintain the Mission profile within the city.

With working relationships, i.e. Reporting to the board of Trustees, for paid and volunteer staff members and to Community Groups, Churches, Council and Government Organisations." (From the Christian Social Services Job Description for the City Missioner.)

And, "Management of the organisation is vested in the role of City Missioner." (From the Governance Policy Updated 2009)

It was a management role with responsibility to develop this social service for the Whanganui community.

Early in my term as City Missioner, I should have required the board to better clarify its governance role because when the roles were blurred between governance and management or tasks not carried out, there was a greater chance of division and chaos.

The services around basic needs, such as foodbanks, friendship meals, Ezee meals, gardens and a place to pop in for a cuppa and a chat (Anne's Place and later Our Space), had served this community well, as did the Furniture Barn and visiting team.

I had dreamed of housing the homeless, something the Mission had on its wish list from the original discussions by the Christian Social Services Interim Trust in December 1990.

I believed that op-shops, as they were known, could bring in much-needed financial support as well as offer furniture, clothing and household items in emergencies. This would assist the other services.

I talked to people around the community, those who had houses and those who didn't, those who had jobs and those who didn't, those who had enough food and those who didn't. I was able to assess what was working well, and what needed to change. I reported this back to the board and changes were approved by the board.

I quickly noticed that not all people have a belief in those things which they do not see, a belief in the existence of objects which are invisible and how they are influenced by them.

Just because I had become used to a faith-based life, (that confident expectation of things that are to come), doesn't mean that others had the same belief.

I reflected on the processes I used in developing management policies and procedures, carefully negotiated and discussed with existing volunteers and staff, who had been doing things a certain way for some years.

I was mindful that most of the people around the Mission were from this community. They had lived here, some of them for all their lives, and I was the newcomer.

Like the *Waimarie*, (Whanganui's river steamer) it was my season and I had a head of steam up for the journey. I felt like a builder, supervising construction and sometimes repairs.

I was feisty and hard-edged when needed. Some areas of the work of the Mission were no longer working as well as they used to, or people had left, and others didn't follow on. I assessed the services based on the answers I gleaned from asking my question, "What did this community need the Mission to be doing that no-one else is doing?"

I also kept in mind a social work model learned in my training:

> "To focus on services that helped improve people's behaviour or circumstances to enable them to once again play a meaningful role within their families, communities and society and to work towards the prevention and elimination of social problems in the community."

> *Adapted from the Model of social work from*
> *Aotearoa New Zealand Association of Social Workers.*

I examined the needs of the city through the social indicators (compiled by the District Council), over past years and the most recent census information. I talked with people in the churches and with city councillors and key people in non-government agencies in the city. I had spoken with young people who wandered Victoria Avenue and I located the sleeping places of the city's homeless, and spent time with them to get their view, expectations and hopes.

I sought and collated any statistics I could find on the people who had come to the Mission since its inception and identified funding that might fit the areas we needed to be working in, both historic sources and new ones, and compiled a funding calendar.

I inherited the role of fundraising and three years of a lack of accountability for previous funds granted.

The previous City Missioner had expressed it this way, "that he never had much interest in funding. He felt that it was the board's job, but they left it to him and the administrator."

By 2006 goals were set and the new directions agreed. These were changes to existing services and planned new services. With clear policies and procedures for each of the core services approved by the board in 2006–2007, we had a clear path from initial interview through to whichever core services were accessed. We were all on the same page. Or were we?

In reporting back to the board and "being accountable to the chairperson for all work undertaken for the board" what more could I have done to ensure I kept on the same page as the board. They didn't see what I saw first-hand, nor did the board sit in the office with me and the staff members listening to the reasons people came to us and how they made decisions that often led them into further difficulties. An ex-board member, the late Dick Mansfield, expressed this so well,

> "How can we, who have so much, really understand the people you work with, who make choices about survival each day. Some of these choices are so different to what I would make."

I remembered the times we sat in my office talking about this as I saw how he struggled to understand some of our clients' decisions.

With improved statistics gathered, we had more accurate information about the people who came to the Mission and the areas where help was needed. With a good knowledge of what other agencies did in the community it was easy to see how we linked with them, referred clients to them and they referred clients to us.

The total number of people who accessed the Mission's services at the end of 2007 was 1,187.

By 2008, the work of the Mission was increasing, remembering this was about the time of a global financial crisis. An increase in the number of paid staff from two to eight enabled us to manage the growing core services. Most of these were young people as I had linked with the WINZ, who offered work subsidies for people who had been out of work for a year or more. These could last from six months to over a year. It was important to be able to sustain these positions after the funding stopped. If a staff member left for another job, we could again apply for the work subsidy if the next person met the criteria. Mostly this was available for people between 20 to 40 years old, so the average age of staff dropped to within this range. Younger people began volunteering because they knew some of these younger staff members.

Younger people had begun volunteering at the Mission to help fill their time, moved into paid employment with us, and then moved on to employment elsewhere. Many expressed how the Mission helped them find confidence and learn skills that enabled them to get employment.

This was also evident in the people referred to us through the Corrections Service to do their Community Service. In the last two years there were around 3,000 contracted to do their community hours at the Mission. This was a service in itself, as they needed supervision, the responsibility for which was delegated to the appropriate manager.

We were doing the necessary food and fellowship through the foodbank, Friendship Meals, Ezee meals, Christmas lunch, Anne's Place and the Travel Club. We were creating opportunities for the possible, through the development of the Garage sale/Furniture Barn/Mission Possible Shop, including possible financial independence. We were doing what had been seen as the impossible through the set-up of the Total Care Budget service and the Project Jericho — Emergency and Temporary Residential Service.

A sense of synergy came upon the Mission. This team of people from very different cultures, experiences and faiths were drawn together and provided an almost seamless delivery of services for people who came to the Mission. I used the word synergy, because the result of working together was greater than the sum of each person's individual effect and capabilities.

The total number of people who accessed the Mission's services at the end of 2008 was 1,567.

In 2009, we had begun the year with a sense of nostalgia, having moved from strength to strength. My role changed to being less like a fire fighter putting out fires, to one of teacher and supervisor as people came and went in the Mission team.

Some came of necessity and others were drawn into this collaborative environment. Even though as a country we had moved into the grip of a recession and the demand on the Mission's services had grown, the team remained committed to the needs of the people who found their way to the Mission.

When the board members changed, I needed to get alongside the new members and better understand their thinking, gifts and skills they brought to the board. I held an orientation after the AGM once a year for existing and new board members, with key staff and some volunteers present. Maybe I could have done more to help them understand the work of the City Mission.

When the board chose its new chairperson, I could have spent more time getting alongside them, as it was required that they, "develop and ongoing and supportive relationship with the City Missioner." (Governance Policy updated 18 May 2009.)

In the latter months of 2009 questioning began, and I believe the focus shifted from synergy and synchronicity to hierarchy, money and self.

Was the Mission about mission to this community or me? For me it had always been about mission, about service to others less fortunate than I was. This would have been a good question to explore together with those who began to push for the change of direction.

It seemed to me, that many people in the churches were no longer interested in the treasure they had created, or they had long forgotten their responsibility to the poor. This was evidenced in the reduction by half of their annual levy from $12,000 in the 1990s from each of the denominations involved, down to $6,000 by 2010.

On the home front, during this unsettling time I was to face personal loss of my Dad, my hero, along with the grief of my mother, just two months short of their 70th wedding anniversary.

I captured some of this in my Column in the *Wanganui Midweek* of 4 November 2009 (their wedding anniversary), entitled, *"It is not a mountain we conquer but ourselves,"* a quote from another man I looked up to, Sir Edmund Hillary.

> "Life is sometimes hard and challenging. For me the last two months have been just that. Today would have been my parents' 70th wedding anniversary, had Dad not died. I had everything planned, the food, invitations, even planned a letter from the Queen. But it wasn't to be. We have interred his ashes instead.
>
> I feel like I have climbed a mountain, my energy is low, I am tired and feel alone and frustrated that I cannot conquer this mountain.
>
> But it isn't a mountain, it is me. I said some columns ago I would take it easy and be kind to myself; well, I confess, I am not good at being kind to me. Some of you will be smiling and saying, "I knew that." And you are right. Sometimes I am my own worst enemy. Sometimes we expect so much more from ourselves that we create an unreachable peak and then feel we have let each other down because we didn't make it up there.
>
> So, I say this Tibetan prayer – Grant that I may be given appropriate difficulties and sufferings on this journey so that my heart might be awakened, and my practice of universal liberation and compassion may be truly fulfilled. Arohanui and Thank you for your support."
>
> *Wanganui Midweek, 4 November 2009.*

The total number of people who accessed the Mission's services at the end of 2009 was 2,067.

During 2010 there were times of peace allowing me to be that active advocate for those most vulnerable in our city and to supervise and support the hardworking team.

Then there were the times when I felt that the direction the board had begun to take was all about control and authority. The importance of the City Missioner's role in influencing the strategic direction based on the needs experienced first-hand in the community, was being diminished.

The overbearing and intrusive behaviour, with constant demands and veiled threats were draining me and the administrator, and I'm sure some members of the board echoed my thoughts. This stressful time continued through the middle of 2010, and then I was informed that there had been a change of chairperson. The strong bureaucratic mind-set and a taking of sides continued amongst attempts to reach agreements.

Finally reaching an agreement through mediation that, "the board would engage a suitable person in the role of Mission Co-ordinator," was a breakthrough. With the board, "accepting full responsibility for the past lack of clear parameters and processes in financial management and acknowledging that as City Missioner I was not encouraging dependency on the Mission by clients," (Letter dated 21 March 2011), the way seemed clear to move forward together.

I was still tasked with delivering the services required to meet the objects of the Trust, even though the Mission Co-ordinator position remained unfilled for some months, causing issues in the funding round for grants the work of the Mission depended on.

There were times when we tried to understand each other, there were peace gestures, (two cakes with white doves on them), which were much appreciated by the staff, and meetings to try to work things through. I believe there was an undercurrent running, resulting in polarisation creating a 'them and us situation.'

When secret meetings took place, transparency was lost, and it became harder to trust each other. A much better model would have been to sit around the table and work through the issues rather than dictate or blame. To find win/win outcomes.

As the City Mission staff and volunteers felt unsupported and not valued, or attacked and belittled by some board members, it seemed to be impossible to continue.

It was interesting that at mediation when we finally sat around the table, with the people who could make decisions, the differences were not that great and had this been done earlier, much of the needed work of the Mission might have been saved.

The board's planned move into a corporate business model, to turn the Mission into an exemplary social work agency, and to restructure was shared with me. It seemed to be without consultation with key stakeholders or staff and volunteers.

The total number of people who accessed the Mission's
services at the end of 2010 was 3,607.

The Mission staff and volunteers struggled to accommodate the increased numbers of people seeking support and care.

There was talk about closing services and in fact by September 2011 to close the City Mission, (because of a lack of funding), and not hold the Christmas Lunch.

This hierarchical approach and the board's endeavour to place an ill-fitting business template across this social service, created distrust and even fear in some parts of the community.

Stories came back from the community that the board believed we were creating dependency in people who turned to the Mission for help.

From September 2011 onwards, the board seemed set on closing the Mission completely. By November it seemed a done deal as the board at a special meeting in November decided the following:

- "cease all volunteer payments

- reduce food parcels to existing and donated stock only

- stop supporting the friendship meals with purchased meat

- cancel the Christmas lunch unless after preparing a budget it was cash positive

- advise staff of restructuring before Christmas

- review Project Jericho with a view to alternative operational options."

This was also an election year and it was a surprise to me how the political arena had crept into the challenges we faced. It became clearer at a gathering of people to meet the then Prime Minister John

Key in Majestic Square. Staff who were Labour supporters and board members who were National supporters faced off.

With all this going on I worked all that much harder at the coal face as I watched the greatest number of clients arrive at the City Mission, 600 more than 2010.

> The total number of people who accessed the Mission's services at the end of 2011 was 4,195.

By the end of December 2011, I was no longer the City Missioner.

During my time at the Mission I had the wonderful opportunity to work with some amazing people and to rub shoulders with talented and committed volunteers and board members, many of whom had served the Mission well during its 20-year journey.

The Mission had been birthed by people of vision who saw the need and knew that care had to be taken to continually build up the monetary reserves to meet any emergency. The work of the City Mission was challenging and stressful and, as City Missioner, I had done the best I could managing the day-to-day operation of core services, training and empowering staff and volunteers.

Respond

Having time to review and reflect on the things that had happened over the seven years, I wondered about what I could have done differently? What could I learn from this experience, and offer to others?

These are my learnings:

- **The importance of clear governance and management policies.**

  Take time to ensure that boards have clear understandings about governance and management. This may prevent divisions and difficulties.

- **Lines of authority between governance and management need to be clearly stated and understood.**

  The limits of the management role and the board's power to act need to be transparent and continually checked out, as policies and new initiatives were introduced.

- **Finance and fundraising responsibilities need to be clearly delineated and lines of accountability accepted by all parties.**

  Raising the money needed to run an organisation is one of the board's governance responsibilities. When concerns about the cost of running an organisation remind the governance group it is their responsibility, the board need to step up. It is their responsibility find the people who have the skills to raise the required funds and to have the checks and balances in place to prevent financial mismanagement.

- **Faith is not the same for everyone.**

  Sharing our individual faith journeys is of great importance to encourage others.

- **A Christian based social service needs to be based on biblical principles.**

  For a Christian based organisation, the parable of the good Samaritan is paramount where Jesus makes it clear that our neighbour is anyone who has a need of our love. We need to tell modern day parables based on those in the Bible.

- **Good communication between management and governance are of the utmost importance.**

  Gossip, innuendo and misunderstandings need to be nipped in the bud and cleared face-to-face, as soon as difficulties start to emerge. Good record keeping, and accurate minutes of meetings are essential. A clear and speedy process for resolving differences is essential. This would allow incorrect information to be clarified as soon as possible.

- **Find ways to bring together the wisdom of older people and the energy of the younger ones.**

  Respecting each person's experience and abilities is essential. We are called to serve many different ages with different experiences.

- **Be open to learning new ways and trying new things.**

  Being set in certain ways and practices limits learning. Certain old ways, e.g. "We tried that 10 years ago and it didn't work then," or "We have always done it this way," make for difficulties in moving forward and experiencing positive growth and change.

- **Always engage with the local council, key stake holders and community people.**

   When little interest is shown, connections with stake holders and those interested in the work need to be established. Links with the Council and government agencies provide a very important way of feeding back information about social needs of the less fortunate in the community.

- **Don't become marginalised.**

   When working with marginalised people it is easy, and unconsciously possible, to also become disregarded and even banished.

- **Corporate business models do not work for social service agencies.**

   While it is important for social services agencies to be run on financially responsible lines, they are not there to make a profit. Being efficient in a social services model means taking the long view of a person's well-being, listening and assessing, without trying to impose quick fix solutions. Relationships are more important than targets for the use of time and money.

- **Believe in yourself.**

   Have good supervision. Don't become overwhelmed or isolated by your unease. I could have made my concerns more public, gathered support from the community, and maybe challenged the perception of the board's dysfunction in a different way. Write letters to people who might be able to make a difference and go public if necessary.

- **How to live your life is your choice.**

   Each decision you make at the time, was the right decision for that time. Sometimes decisions are well researched and negotiated with all stake holders. Sometimes decisions are made in the middle of crisis, life and death situations, that often involve people that struggled to keep themselves and their families safe.

   I learned to choose joy and peace in the middle of these circumstances because things will always change. The next minute, hour or day would be seen differently. For now, this is your decision. Without the hard times, life would be unbalanced, and we might not appreciate the times of joy and peace.

Now was time to restore my life.

Epilogue

The cycle closed leaving questions to be answered:

1. Who cares for the underprivileged if this polarisation were to continue?

2. Who would notice the huge gap between those who are comfortable and those who are struggling?

3. How will people find hope in our city and be able to dream, dreams?

Other groups have picked up some of what the Mission used to do.

In December 2011, I penned my last column in the *Wanganui Midweek*. I had been told that I could no longer write as the City Missioner, hence the disclaimer at the beginning.

"This is NOT the City Missioner's Column — The views expressed here are not those of the Christian Social Services Board. Titled, *"And who is my neighbour?"* from Luke Chapter 10: verse 29. I wrote:

> "While travelling down a road, a man was attacked, his belongings taken, and his clothes torn. The attackers beat him up very badly and left him lying and bleeding on the side of the road. Two men walked past him lying on the side of the road; one crossed over to the other side, so as to act like he didn't notice the beaten man; the second slowed down a little but left without helping him.
>
> A third man walked along the road and this man saw the beaten and bruised body, hardly breathing; he felt compassion for the beaten man, tended his wounds and carried him to a place to stay and paid for him until he got better; even promising to come back and pay any extra costs at a later date.
>
> Which of the three men do you think was a neighbour to the man who was left beaten on the side of the road?
>
> The one who had compassion and helped him. Jesus told him, "Go and do the same." Seven years and 384 columns later – the question and answer are still the same for me. We must have compassion – Go and do the same. No matter how hard it is, or how many people agree or disagree with me.

In the words of John Wesley, we are invited to: "Do all the good you can. By all the means you can. In all the ways you can. In all the places you can. At all the times you can. To all the people you can. As long as ever you can." This truth has not changed for me. Arohanui.

Wanganui Midweek, December 2011.

Remembering the words attributed to John Wesley helped me to remember what this was really about – serving people. Or in the words of the Māori proverb:

He aha te mea nui o te ao.
What is the most important thing in the world?

He tāngata, he tāngata, he tāngata.
It is the people, it is the people, it is the people.

For me it was always about the most vulnerable people in our community.

I was out of the Mission, but the debate continued.

On 23 April 2012 under "Your View" in the *Wanganui Chronicle* a piece entitled *"Board must go"* – John Penny an ex-board member and a volunteer at Project Jericho shared his concern:

> "Having attended many years of AGM's at Christian Social Services (CSSW) charitable organisation, I can only conclude that the board – which has been described as inept, delusional and dysfunctional by previous board members and management – can only save "grace" by resigning. They have let down the churches they represent and more importantly, the needy of this great little city. The last few years they have agonised over such decisions as a new mission statement working towards a more "holistic approach" and other "garbage" such as a business model where each section makes a profit.
>
> The need in our society for CSSW has grown rapidly, and each year a budget of some $300,000 is required through charitable organisations/government grants/goodwill of donators. The churches only contribute $36,000 therefore, close to 90 per cent of funding comes from other sources, as well as funds raised from the shop and charges for some services, such as accommodation.
>
> The board's fundraising efforts have been nil and, even worse have shown a loss. Their lack of success has obviously meant that there

is nothing left to fill the food parcels with fresh food, there is no ability to pay what has been a loyal band of experienced, dedicated staff.

Any constructive criticism of the board has been met with almost outright anger, and I can only conclude this "siege mentality" comes from a collective guilty conscience. Even the Christmas dinner was to be cancelled until the City Missioner got the money from the community at the last minute (we know what her reward was for years of dedication to the organisation was).

From the ashes of what was a worthwhile Christian charity some years ago may rise something that better fits the needs of the desperate in our society. Of course, the architects of its demise must face up and step aside."

On 27 April 2012, David W A Bennett – Pacific Helmets (NZ) Ltd, wrote in the *Wanganui Chronicle* "Your View" that: *"Board must stay."*

Another letter on 30 April 2012 from Mike Pyefinch, an ex-staff member made redundant from Managing Project Jericho, speaks to the contrary, *"Board must go."* (See below.)

Some board members did resign and so I understand did David Bennett not long afterwards. Mike Pyefinch is again working with those people struggling to find a place to live in these difficult times, in Wellington.

I had read the articles in the *Wanganui Chronicle*, *River City Press* and *Wanganui Midweek* about the Mission.

My son, his wife and I watched with despondency as the shop was closed, and read an article quoting

Board must stay

I'm not sure which meeting your correspondent John A Penney (*Chronicle*, April 23) attended recently, but it obviously wasn't the one I attended, where in particular the chairman, Tim Campbell, (and the board by implication) received spontaneous applause at the end of the meeting. Tim deserves a medal for the burden he has carried for the last 12 months.

I would also suggest that Mr Penney should be careful as to who he describes as "inept", "delusional", and "dysfunctional". These are not descriptive words used by the church that appoints and supports me as board member, and perhaps he may wish to speak to actual mission board members before parroting off on hearsay information that is wide of the mark.

The people of Wanganui can be very grateful that the City Mission board has acted in the way that it has. And hopefully, with wide public support, we will be able to continue to run a quality free Foodbank and other services as part of a Christian response to local needs.

DAVID W A BENNETT
Pacific Helmets (NZ) Ltd

the Chairperson who claimed, "… it [the shop] lost $30,000–$40,000 a year and could have continued if it was cash neutral." *Wanganui Chronicle, 27 January 2012.* The best of the stock was on sold to other shops.

The shop was reopened after two months, renamed the City Mission Shop and moved yet another couple of times. We saw the truck we presumed to be owned by the Mission doing pick-ups and deliveries.

I remembered that I had asked the board to raise funds for a truck with a lift on the back many times over several years only to be told, "No!" It would have made a huge difference to the goods being picked up and delivered. The trailer was seen at a board member's house and at their place of business almost out of sight for months, rusting away.

As a family we supported each other through the gossip and the incorrect information that travelled around the community over the next two years. Times were hard, but we got by, we had each other.

When questions were being asked about the City Missioner role and if it would be replaced, a *River City Press* write up, dated 9 February 2012 quoting Board member Miles Bockett said,

Board must go

What David Bennett fails to make clear in his defence of CSSW board chairman Tim Campbell (Letters, April 27), citing a "spontaneous round of applause" he received at the AGM, was that it was preceded by a sustained barrage of questioning from concerned community members over board ineptitude that was never answered.

The applause was not widespread and was called for by board members, presumably in the hope of endorsing their mismanagement. I have worked for the past two years as a supervisor at Project Jericho so have a clear understanding of the labels Mr Bennett seems so offended by, so let's break it down:

Inept — Taking the task of fundraising off the person who had a clear knowledge and success with it and giving it to someone who didn't understand the process and failed.

Delusional — The only visible fundraising effort of the board made a loss of $835.

Dysfunctional — Dedicating enormous time and money on removing the City Missioner, in the belief that the mission could remain effective without her level of knowledge, experience and expertise. Shedding the emergency accommodation and the four staff, whose workload was never understood by the board, is testament to this dysfunction.

How long is it to be before the Foodbank is forced to limit the service it provides?

Tim Campbell does not deserve a medal, rather the community deserves his — and the rest of the board's — acknowledgment of failure and resignation.

MIKE PYEFINCH
Wanganui

> "…while the board returns operations to normal, the role of City Missioner, currently vacant, may be assisted by local clergy of the four churches who form the basis of CSSW…It may be in future the role is disestablished."

I watched the community and churches, who were not affiliated to the Mission fill some of the gaps left by the services the board closed.

Then the long wait for a place for the homeless. I offered my experience and skills, but they were not needed. More than once I received calls from people desperate for somewhere to live and was able, with my now limited means, to find something for them.

I maintained my commitments to people who had asked me to continue to support them, some of whom I am still in regular contact with.

I see very few statistics and hear very little of what is done by the Mission these days.

For me this was an awful experience. None of the work I had done before in prisons, drug and alcohol detox facilities and the Probation Service had been so stressful and demoralising.

Months of erosion of the job I loved and invested my heart in, employment action for a second time against the board, the outcomes of unresolved complaints generated from the last few months at the Mission, which went on until January 2016, were finally resolved through mediation.

I certainly had experienced being in the wilderness.

Now, for those of you who think this kind of cycle was only happening in Whanganui, I invite you to read a newspaper article from *The Dominion Post* on Thursday 14 March 2013 titled, *"City Mission lacks heart, says ex-leader"* which quotes the Anglican Bishop of Wellington, Justin Duckworth – "Mrs Blakie was an amazing woman, but had clearly found parts of her job frustrating." This was followed in March 2013 with two letters to the Editor.

In a letter to the Editor in *The Dominion Post* on 22 March 2013 titled *"Former mission trustees respond…"* from Graham Stewart, Chairman 1991–1994 and Warren Allen, Chairman 2005–2009 who wrote:

"We are alarmed to read City Mission lacks a heart, says ex-leader (14 March). The City Mission was set up in 1904 and since, has had nine City Missioners who have served Wellington and its citizens with dedication.

In recent years, it moved to set up divisions for all needs; mission for youth, transition to work, mission for independence, foodbank, the drop-in centre, budgeting and money management advice, mission for seniors and 'Ezee' meals. The mission has, for more than 100 years, cared for citizens across the age spectrum, thanks to the business community and caring Wellingtonians. Without their help, it wouldn't have happened. The marriage of mission staff within an organisation in which diverse skills are needed, has always been managed by the trustees with professionalism, the chief executive handling the operations business side and the missioner working at the coalface. They've always worked as a team. Over the years, trustees have been there to support the missioner of the day and staff. It's a community with warmth and understanding, all working for the same goal. We found this article most distressing."

And then another letter appeared in *The Dominion Post*, dated 28 March 2013, written by Sheila Reed entitled, *"They were kinder gentler times."* She wrote:

"Graham Stewart's comment (Letters 22 March) brought back fond memories of when he chaired the board of Wellington City Mission. Those were kinder, happier days. Staff noticed immediately when the business model was adopted, and the first chief executive appointed – a chilly wind of change. Many of us immediately organised ourselves a collective, with a union's help, to afford ourselves some protection. It was heart breaking to watch the office of City Missioner being slowly eroded until it was totally subordinated to the chief executive; we went from a time when the Missioner was vital to policy-making and deciding future directions to a time when they were excluded and discouraged.

And of course, a top-down management also undervalues its staff, who, in turn, become discouraged. It's hard to see how the next Missioner will fit into the current structure. Let's hope and pray the pendulum swings back soon."

It sounded all very familiar to me, as did these comments from Judge Andrew Becroft. From a story by Jade Reidy in the *SPANZ magazine* Autumn 2018 issue. She wrote:

"When Andrew Becroft attended the Rātana Church's annual celebrations in January 2018, the Children's Commissioner experienced a homecoming. As a committed Christian whose first appointment to the bench was the Whanganui District Court in 1996, Andrew says the city and its people have a special place in his heart. "I was judicially born and nurtured a judge there." Whanganui also is where Andrew realised that the most troublesome teenagers weren't just naughty; the youth court was dealing with the most marginalised and alienated young people in the country. Too many of them were Maori. "Most New Zealanders don't know how terrible it really is at the bad end," he says. "While 70 percent of children are doing well, 20 percent struggle and 10 percent are doing badly, it's deeply concerning."

This was the same Whanganui I was City Missioner in for just over seven years, working 70+ hours most weeks, alongside the dedication of 100 volunteers and 10 paid staff endeavouring to meet the needs of some 15,000 clients and their families. It was an impossible task, but we did our best.

I found a smile amongst my tears as I read the newspaper article and letters. The smile, because it wasn't only about me, and a tear because again the most vulnerable in our communities are marginalised with this kind of behaviour.

As the days became months and the months became years, I began to see light again, to find my beloved brother Jesus in the eyes of people I met and chose to serve in a new way. I found my Divine Creator in the beauty of nature, in the sparkling waters that nurtured me back to health, and the hands of loved family and friends.

As the months passed, I watched the creamy moons that hovered over my house, often surrounded by sparkling stars. I remembered how magnificent life really is.

When gentle raindrops fell on me they reminded me I am washed and renewed. In the struggles and tears of life we can be washed and renewed.

I began to smile again and recognised my angels and guides waiting beside me for my invitation to be healed, to grieve what I have lost, and now to complete this episode in my life.

I have lived through this challenge and learned so much about myself and others. I have changed the things I could change, and now enable others to take the risk of facing truth and welcoming change. Let's not forget to hope and pray.

This is now another episode in my life of miracles and you have had a front row seat.

Acknowledgements

To my family both blood and chosen I am grateful for your belief in me.

Especially the 'girls' who became readers, carers of correctness, challenging of my sentence structure and grammar setting me straight.

To Tony, thank you for your years of support through our team ministry and especially through these difficult times.

To Shiloh my ever present furry friend, sat at my feet sharing his strong caring energy. You hung in beside me until your death the week of finishing the book.

Glossary

CSSW – Christian Social Services Wanganui

Deacon and Presbyter – Definitions from the Methodist Law Book
MINISTERS –

2. 1 A Presbyter is one who is ordained by the Methodist Church of
New Zealand to the particular ministry of Word, Sacrament, and
Pastoral Care and to leadership within the community of faith.

2. 2 A Deacon is one who is ordained by the Methodist Church of
New Zealand to a ministry shaped by the community whom they
are appointed to serve.

Department of Social Welfare

Restructured 1 May 1992 into business units:

- New Zealand Income Support Service

- New Zealand Children and Young Persons Service

- New Zealand Community Funding Agency

- Social Policy Agency

- Corporate Office

1 October 1998: Department of Work and Income (branded as
Work and Income New Zealand or **WINZ**) established with the
merger of Income Support with the New Zealand Employment
Service, Community Employment Group and Local Employment
Co-ordination.

1 October 1999: Ministry of Social Policy established, with the
amalgamation of the Social Policy Agency and Corporate Office
functions of the former Department of Social Welfare and the
addition of the new Purchasing and Monitoring Group.

1 October 1999: Department of Child, Youth and Family Services
(**CYFS**) established. Was previously Children, Young Persons and
their Families Agency (**CYPFA**).

1 October 2001: Ministry of Social Development established with the amalgamation of the Ministry of Social Policy and the Department of Work and Income.

1 July 2006: Child, Youth and Family becomes a service line of the Ministry of Social Development (**CYF**).

Ecumenical is a term used in church circles that means promoting unity of different churches and groups, the same term used in a universal sense means involving all people or groups.

Housing Ministry

1974: State Advances Corporation merges with Housing Division of the Ministry of Works to become Housing Corporation of New Zealand (replacing National Housing Council of New Zealand).

1992 Housing Corporation of New Zealand split to form: Housing Corporation of New Zealand, Housing New Zealand Ltd, Ministry of Housing.

1994 Community Housing Ltd formed as a subsidiary of Housing Corporation of New Zealand

1998 Portions of responsibility of Ministry of Housing transferred to Ministry of Social Policy

2001 Housing Corporation of New Zealand (HCNZ) merged with Housing New Zealand Ltd and Community Housing Ltd, together with housing policy staff from Ministry of Social Policy, to form the Housing New Zealand Corporation (HNZ).

2006 Housing New Zealand Corporation administers Housing Innovation demonstration fund established to fund third sector social housing.

2011 Responsibility for funding third sector social housing moved to the independent Social Housing Unit with support from the Department of Building and Housing. Policy function moved from Housing New Zealand Corporation to the Department of Building and Housing.

2014 Responsibility for managing applications, assessing eligibility for social housing and administering income-related rents is transferred from Housing New Zealand Corporation to the Ministry of Social Development, to help ensure all social housing providers are on an equal footing.

Maslow's Hierarchy

"Abraham Maslow's original hierarchy of needs model was developed between 1943 –1954. His 1943 paper was described as a theory in psychology titled "A theory of Human Motivation." Maslow used the terms "physiological," "safety," "belonging" and "love," "esteem," "self-actualisation," and "self-transcendence" to describe the pattern that human motivations generally move through." *Abbreviated from Wikipedia*

MSD – Ministry of Social Development. 1 October 2001 – the Ministry of Social Development was established with the amalgamation of the Ministry of Social Policy and the Department of Work and Income.

Theology of 'social responsibility.' Defined in Investopedia as the idea that businesses should balance profit-making activities with activities that benefit society. It involves developing businesses with a positive relationship to the society in which they operate.

TCB: Total care Budget

Wanganui to Whanganui: Although called Wanganui from 1854, the New Zealand Geographic Board recommended the name be changed to "Whanganui," and the government decided in December 2009 that, while either spelling was acceptable, Crown agencies would use the Whanganui spelling. The different spellings arose from the way in which local iwi pronounce the word 'Whanganui' (the 'wh' creating a barely aspirated sound) and the way in which European settlers wrote down the word as they heard it ('Wanganui').

Index

P

R

S

T

W

www.ingramcontent.com/pod-product-compliance
Lightning Source LLC
Chambersburg PA
CBHW070113260726
48658CB00001B/96

9 781725 629141